What on Earth You Can Do with Kids

by
Robyn Freedman Spizman
and
Marianne Daniels Garber, Ph.D.

illustrated by Veronica Terrill

Cover by Janet Skiles

Copyright © Good Apple, 1991

ISBN No. 0-86653-623-X

Printing No. 987654321

Good Apple
1204 Buchanan St., Box 299
Carthage, IL 62321-0299

SIMON & SCHUSTER A Paramount Communications Company

Dedication

To our earthlings who make our world go round. . . Justin and Ali
Amy, Arielle and Adam.

Table of Contents

GA1342

Introduction

What on Earth You Can Do with Kids is your comprehensive guide to a year-long focus on the environment. With exciting activities, imaginative bulletin boards, hands-on experiments, purposeful art projects and a multitude of earth-shaking ideas, this book is jam packed with projects and units that will keep you and your students well-grounded throughout the school year. In the process your students will learn the basics that informed earthlings must know to preserve the earth. Given this information, your students will be ready and willing to put into motion many actions that can and will make a difference to our environment. As the movers and shakers of tomorrow, they will lead their parents and friends to a better world today.

Centered around environmental concerns, the basic earth-related concepts are presented from September through May with a personal glossary of Earth Words. Organized by months, each concept is explained and then reinforced through interrelated Earthly Ideas, Earthly Activities and Earth to Homework. Each month brings timely topics offering specific themes around which you can build and integrate your studies. With materials reflecting varied skill levels, this comprehensive book is your year-long environmental guide developed with grades one to five in mind.

The seasons of fall, winter and spring alert students to earthly concerns fundamental to an understanding of the environment. Students are introduced to the interrelationships among animals, plants and the environment called the ecosystem. Fall heralds an earthly welcome cautioning students about the demand for conservation of earth's resources and continues through the year with energy-innovating activities to preserve the earth. Winter and spring continue the focus with illuminating projects focusing on endangered species, energy production and consumption, pesticides, recycling, global warming and acid rain. Throughout the months each concept is presented through bulletin boards, class activities, projects and homework. From readiness skills to independent projects, students are challenged to participate in saving the earth's wonders as the pages unfold.

Your natural concern for the environment will influence all our lives as you prepare your students to carefully consider their impact on the earth's treasures. Teachers are the core of the earth, and we thank you for being among the world's greatest!

GA1342

What on Earth You Can Do in

September

1

GA1342

Earth Words for September

At first glance, many of these concepts appear difficult for children in the primary grades, but we're quite confident that your young earthlings are not only up to the assignment but they probably are already aware of many of these terms! Survey your students understanding of these terms:

Natural Resource: The natural wealth of an area including land, mineral deposits, forests, water supplies and other usable resources found in the area

Observer: Someone who carefully watches and listens to what he sees and hears

Tree: A tree is the largest of all living plants; it has a woody trunk that can stand by itself.

Bark: The bark is the outer layer or skin of the tree. It forms a hard tissue that protects the living parts of the tree.

Conservation: The cautious use of natural resources so they are not misused or used up

Environment: The air, water, minerals and all external factors that affect an organism

Botanist: A scientist who studies plants

Leaf: The leaves are green attachments to the branches of trees which have the job of making food for the tree.

Roots: The roots are the long underground branches of a tree that anchor the tree in the ground and collect water and minerals from the soil.

Photosynthesis: The process during which plants use sunlight to transform carbon dioxide, water and other minerals into food

Oxygen: A colorless, odorless gas given off by plants and needed for life by human beings

Carbon Dioxide: A gas exhaled by human beings and used by plants during photosynthesis

Cycle: A sequence of events that repeatedly reoccurs

GA1342

Mixed-Up Vocabulary

Unscramble the vocabulary words below; then use one to complete each sentence.

CIycE _____   SisSYntePhoOth _____

xygOne _____   stoor _____

kraB _____   TaconResivon _____

venroniment _____   brocAn eidoXiD _____

1. One _____ is the occurrence of morning, afternoon, evening and night every twenty-four hours.

2. When the tree fell over, you could see its _____.

3. With _____, our country could use less oil.

4. Every animal needs _____ to live.

5. _____ is the process through which plants make food.

6. The outer skin of the tree trunk is called _____.

7. Our _____ is everything around us.

8. Plants use the _____ we give off after we breathe in oxygen.

GA1342

Here's the ideal bulletin board to welcome your students at the beginning of the school year. Encourage each child to notice his environment, focusing specifically on trees. Cover the bulletin board with newspaper and cut out pictures from used magazines to emphasize products that come from trees. Duplicate a tree for each child, adding the student's name.

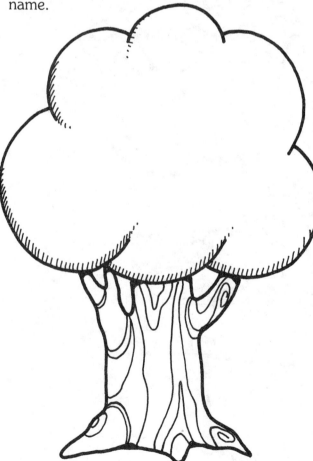

Earthly Ideas

Tree Talk: Have a class discussion about trees and what comes from trees. All trees are plants and need sunlight, air and water. There are thousands of different kinds of trees. What kinds can your class name?

Tree Walk: Take a walk around the school campus. How many different trees do you see? How do they differ? Have students draw the trees and take a photo of each kind.

Make Your Bulletin Board Grow: Students can add products made from trees, photographs and drawings to enhance the board.

Helping Hands for Trees: Have each student trace and cut out a handprint from construction paper and add names of trees, ideas for saving trees and products from trees to enhance the board.

GA1342

A "Tree"mendous Welcome

Use this bulletin board to stress appreciation for the earth's resources and the need to recycle. Add a new title and the tag below to recycle the previous bulletin board and make your point. Enjoy the time and energy saved with new activities.

"Leaf" It to the Leaves

veins

blade

stem

vein: tiny network that moves food product

blade: broad part of the leaf containing food-making cells

stem: attaches leaf to tree

Earthly Ideas

Leaf Talk: Look out the window; take a walk around the grounds. What have your students noticed about the earth as fall days roll through? Record cooler temperatures. Note what time it gets dark each evening. Take a walk to collect earth's castoffs. "Leaf" It to the Leaves: Make a new colorful border for the bulletin board with the leaves students collect. Sandwich each set of leaves between two precut pieces of wax paper. After an adult irons the sheets, students can trim each page to the leaf shape. Use these to make a border.

Collect and Classify: Look at each leaf. How are they alike and different? How many leaves have lobes? Do some have smooth edges and are others serated? Did anyone find any needle-shaped leaves? What colors are the leaves? Why? Are there any evergreen leaves? Classify each leaf as to shape and kind. Cover each with a sheet of construction paper and have the students make leaf rubbings for each kind. Help them to identify each; then compile the pages into a tree book for each pupil to take home.

5

Each month use a small bulletin board covered with newspaper as a current events center. Make the borders out of pictures of endangered species and environmental topics students have collected from newspapers and magazines. Assign environmental topics and encourage students to consult a variety of media sources. Topics might include endangered species, recycling trash, landfills, chemical wastes, etc.

Earthly Projects: Inform your students that they are investigative journalists. Charge them to scour the school and neighborhood looking for environmental issues that need to be addressed. Use the heading on the next page to create a class newsletter, *The Earthling Gazette*. The student-produced newspaper could be sent home monthly to alert parents of school-wide projects on recycling. Student-produced articles informing parents about major concerns, illustrations and class language experience stories could be included.

GA1342

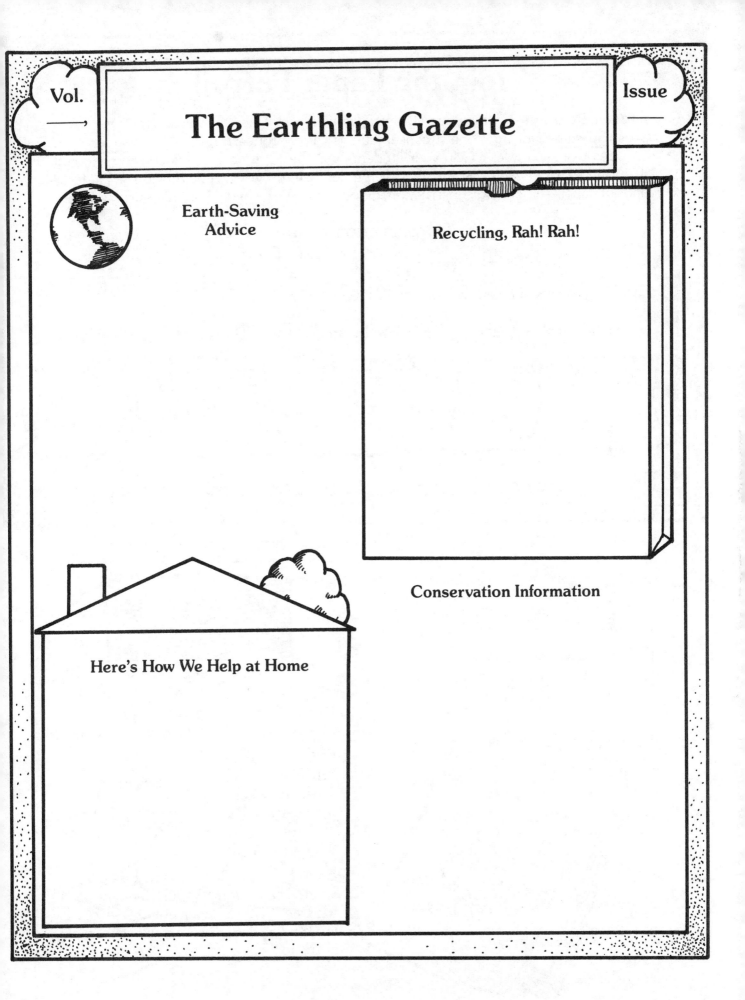

Vol. ____ ,

Issue ____

The Earthling Gazette

Earth-Saving
Advice

Recycling, Rah! Rah!

Conservation Information

Here's How We Help at Home

7

GA1342

Join the Paper Patrol!

Initiate a discussion of where paper comes from. Trees! When we waste paper, we waste trees. So step right up to be a conservationist. First concern: How much paper does the class use each week? Help your students use the form below to keep a class count of the paper used each day for a week. Remember throwaways count, too. Include all kinds of paper—notebook, construction, dittos, work sheets and computer—in your totals.

Conservation Counter

_____'s Conservation Counter

How many sheets of paper did you use this week?

| **Monday** | **Tuesday** | **Wednesday** | **Thursday** | **Friday** |

Totals: _____

Grand Total: _____

- -

Paper Skyscraper: For one week, stack all the used sheets in the front of the classroom. Guess how tall it will be by

Friday. _____ Actual height

of stack on Friday. _____

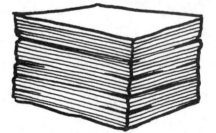

Brainstorming Session: How many ways can the class think of to use less paper?

What would happen to the number of sheets of paper used if each student used both sides of every sheet of paper? If you can't reduce the actual pages, can you think of good uses for them?

Earthly Tip: Recycle used paper as scratch pads for math and telephone pads for Dad. With a paper cutter, cut paper into 3" x 5" (7.6 x 12.7 cm) stacks. Staple at the top.

_____'s Good Earth Deeds

Earthly Idea: What is a good deed? Can you write a sentence about or draw a picture of three good deeds you did this week?

1   2   3

Most of the time when we think of good deeds, we think of helping our fellow earthlings. We can also do good deeds for the planet Earth and all its inhabitants. What are some good deeds you can do for planet Earth?

Good Deeds for the Land

Good Deeds for Animals

Good Deeds for the Oceans

Good Deeds for Energy Use

9

GA1342

Plant Your Thoughts Here

We depend on many plants for things we need. Some plants satisfy our hunger, others give us medicine and still others contain natural fibers that we use to make clothes. Trees give us lumber and paper.

We depend on plants in other ways, too. All plants use carbon dioxide and give off oxygen. We need oxygen to breathe. Plants are very helpful to us. Circle the plants below that we can eat. Draw a square around the ones that we use to make cloth. Put a triangle around any that we use for medicine, and put an X on any plants that give us the raw materials to make things.

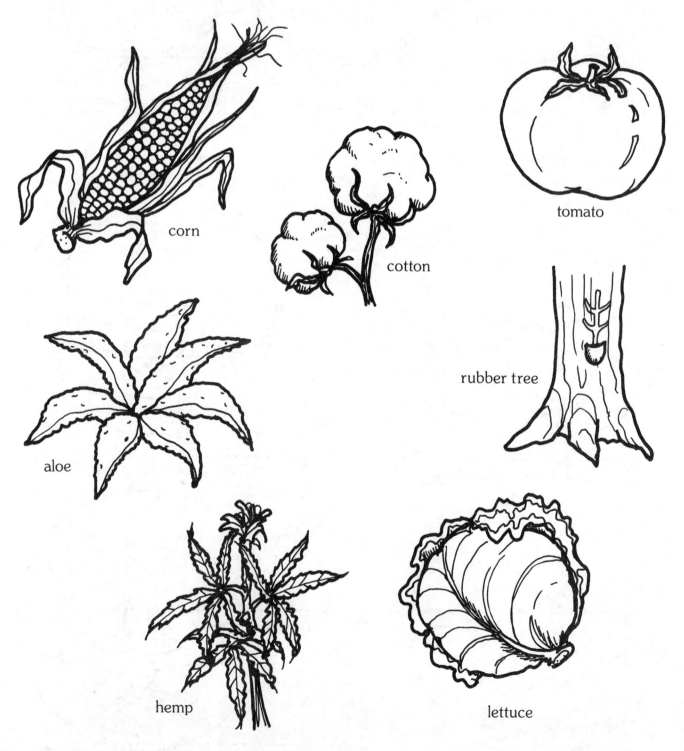

corn

cotton

tomato

aloe

rubber tree

hemp

lettuce

10

Plant on It

Earthly Idea: Plants play an important role on earth. They grow by taking energy from the sun. They use the carbon dioxide that humans and animals exhale in the air and the water and minerals from the ground to grow. Decaying plants enrich the soil for more plants to thrive. In return plants give us food and raw materials and they give off oxygen that we can breathe.

Earthly Activity: Fill in the spaces below to explain how plants are part of the cycle of nature.

What do plants need from man to grow?

What do plants need from the sun?

What do plants get from the soil?

What do plants give off that man needs to live?

GA1342

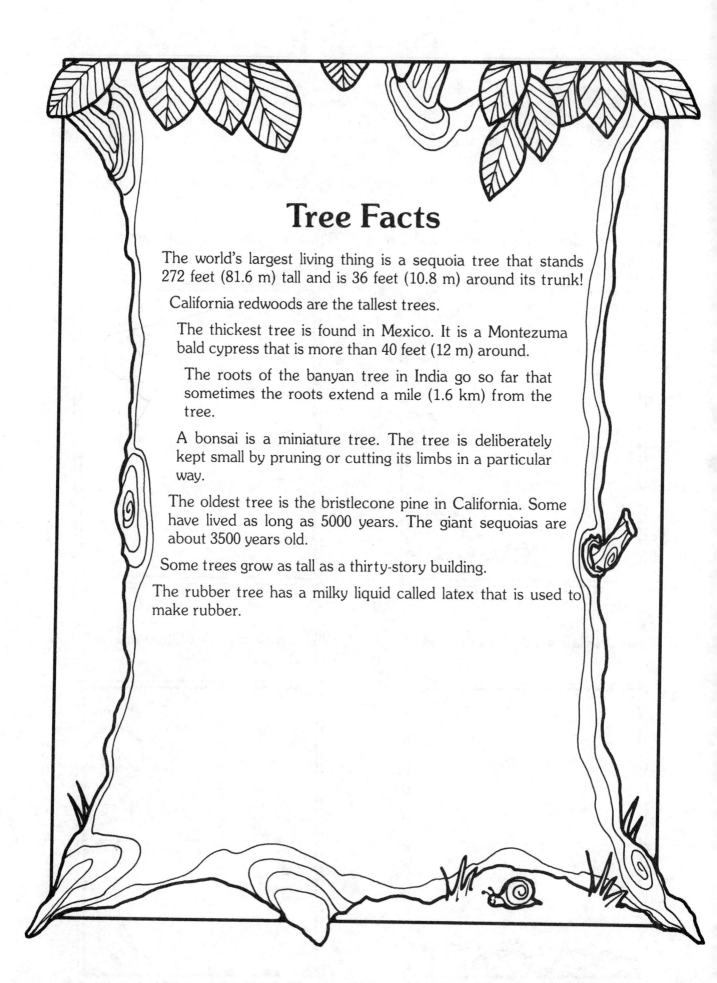

Tree Facts

The world's largest living thing is a sequoia tree that stands 272 feet (81.6 m) tall and is 36 feet (10.8 m) around its trunk!

California redwoods are the tallest trees.

The thickest tree is found in Mexico. It is a Montezuma bald cypress that is more than 40 feet (12 m) around.

The roots of the banyan tree in India go so far that sometimes the roots extend a mile (1.6 km) from the tree.

A bonsai is a miniature tree. The tree is deliberately kept small by pruning or cutting its limbs in a particular way.

The oldest tree is the bristlecone pine in California. Some have lived as long as 5000 years. The giant sequoias are about 3500 years old.

Some trees grow as tall as a thirty-story building.

The rubber tree has a milky liquid called latex that is used to make rubber.

GA1342

Please Help Trees

Earthly Activity: Sometimes trees have to be cut down so other trees can grow well. When there are too many trees in one spot there is not enough sunlight water or nutrients for all of them to grow well. The process of cutting some trees to help other trees is called *thinning*.

Find your way through the maze below by "thinning" the trees that cross the path you want to take.

13

GA1342

Walk and Talk About Trees

Earthly Activity: How many kinds of trees grow on your school's property? Take a walk around the school. Look at each tree. In which category of tree does each seem to fit. Write the name of each tree in the correct box. Paste a leaf of each kind of tree you find in the appropriate category. Will you have all six kinds of trees? See page 19 for more help.

	Broadleaf Trees		**Needleleaf Trees**		**Palms**
	_____		_____		_____

Glue leaf here.	Glue leaf here.	Glue leaf here.

	Cycad Trees		**Tree Ferns**		**Ginkgo Trees**
	_____		_____		_____

Glue leaf here.	Glue leaf here.	Glue leaf here.

GA1342

How to Plant a Tree

Earthly Idea: Trees die every day from disease, natural disasters, drought and by man cutting them down. It is important that we replace the trees that are lost each year.

Earthly Idea: Have the class plant a tree for Arbor Day.

Follow these instructions to plant a tree so it will have the best chance of surviving. First select a tree that will grow well in your region of the country.

Dig a hole big enough for the roots to spread out. Pile the topsoil on one side and the subsoil on the other. If you need to stake the tree, do it now.

Plant the tree. Carefully spread the roots and cover with topsoil. Put the subsoil on top of the hole.

Take care of the tree. Water the tree during the first year while the roots are taking hold. You may need to wrap the trunk with burlap to protect it from too much sun and insects.

GA1342

What Is Your State's Tree?

Every state in the United States has adopted a tree. What is your state's tree? Do you know what it looks like? Look on the map and find your state and color it in. Draw your state tree in the frame below.

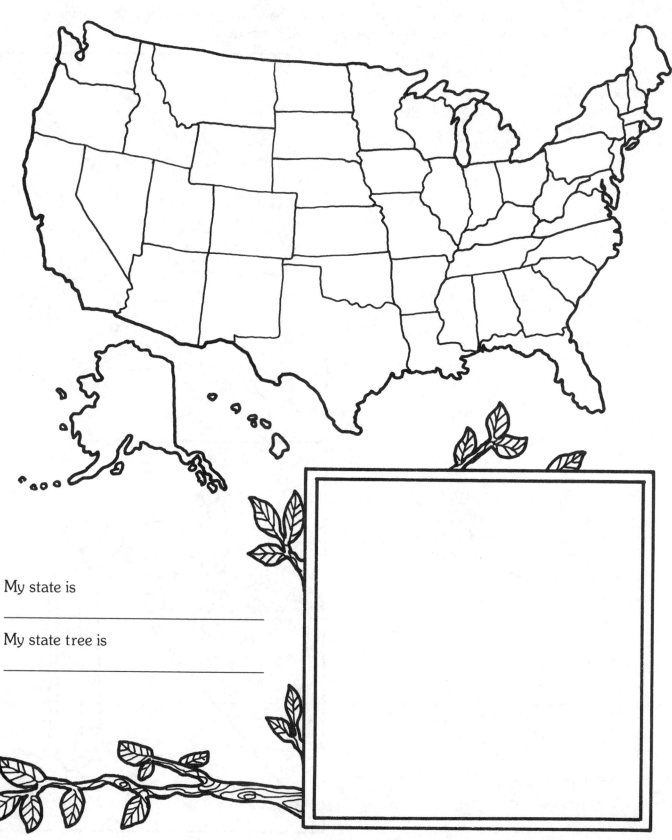

My state is

_____

My state tree is

_____

16

GA1342

Trees Have Seen a Lot

Earthly Idea: A tree usually grows one new layer of wood a year. If you cut a tree in half, the layers of wood look like rings. By counting the rings you can tell how old a tree is.

Earthly Activity: Look at the tree below.

How many rings does it have? _____

What year is it now? _____

In what year would this tree have been planted? _____

Very narrow rings mean a tree was deprived of moisture or sunlight. During what years

of this tree's life did it not grow very much? _____

Can you see the scallops in the rings? Wherever there is a scallop, there was a branch on the tree.

17

GA1342

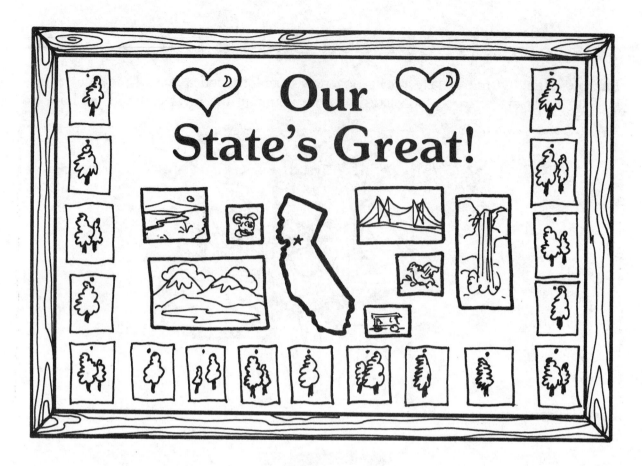

This is a perfect bulletin board to introduce a study of your state. Border the bulletin board with the students' drawings of the state tree. In the center of the board put pictures of your state's natural resources and special attractions.

If the school property happens to have a sample of the state tree, let your children sketch the tree. Talk about its special features. Some children may want to find additional information about why this tree was chosen to represent the state.

18

More Tree Talk

Did you know there are six main kinds of trees?

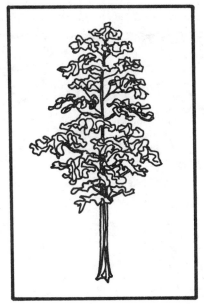

Broadleaf Trees
Broadleaf trees are known for their autumn colors, bare branches in winter and spring flowers.

Needleleaf Trees
Needleleaf trees have needlelike leaves and cones. They are often green all year long.

Palms
Palms are usually tropical trees with huge leaves and no branches.

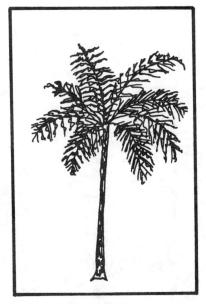

Cycad Trees
Cycad trees live only in warm places like Africa. They have heavy big cones 3 feet (.91 m) long.

Tree Ferns
Tree ferns have no flowers, fruits or seeds. They reproduce by spores.

Ginkgo Trees
Ginkgo trees have seeds but no fruits or cones. The seeds smell very badly.

Tree Talk

How much do you know about trees? There are about 20,000 kinds of trees on earth. More than 1000 kinds grow in the United States. Scientists who study trees and plants are called *botanists*.

Fill in the names of the parts of the tree below: trunk, leaf, root, ring, bark.

GA1342

Fall "Leaves" Me Busy!

Use this bulletin board to be aware of the seasonal changes and how leaves can be recycled. Use the fun art projects on the next page "Like It or Leaf It" to keep your students filled with a fall focus. Other ideas include displaying students' poems, stories and illustrations all about leaves.

Color and complete this note. Take it home to your family.

Ideas to Write Home About

Dear _____ :

A compost is a simple thing
Into a hole the leaves you fling.
Add organic trash,
grass clippings, too.
Combine them all;
It's easy to do.

You won't need fertilizer;
Your garden will thrive;
Our family can help
Mother Earth to survive!

Like It or "Leaf" It,

_____
(Earthling student's name)

GA1342

Like It or "Leaf" It

Leaf People: Trace leaf shapes and add human features to make a family of leaves come to life.

Leaf Prints: Have each student collect four or five leaves from his/her yard. Cover the work area with newspaper. Have each student paint one side of each leaf with tempera paint. Fold a 9″ x 12″ (22.8 x 30.4 cm) sheet of construction paper in half and open it like a book. Place the painted leaves paint-side up on the right side of the page. Close the cover and press the cover to make your prints appear. Now vary the position and overlap the shapes making new images.

Leaf Splatter: Place leaves on top of construction paper. Recycle an old toothbrush or paintbrush by dipping it into paint and splattering the paint onto the paper covered with leaves. This makes great wrapping paper when done on brown roll paper or discarded grocery bags.

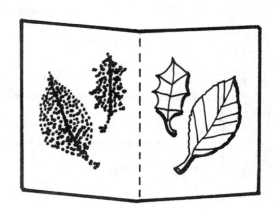

Leaf Matchmaker: Have each student collect two leaves from an identified tree in his/her yard. Bring to class and put one leaf in a pile with other students' leaves. Ready, set, go. Have each student search for his leaf's mate. Staple the pair on the bulletin board adding a label.

OAK

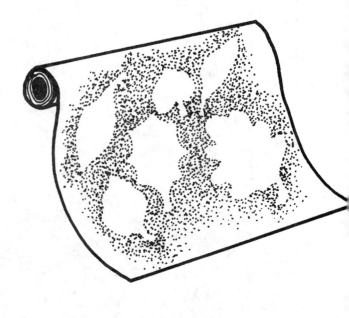

22

Reading Is out of This World!

Here's the perfect bulletin board to encourage students to read books about the environment, space or any subject earth related. For a clever book report, duplicate the Reading Is out of This World activity sheet and instruct students to answer who, what, when, where and why. When students read a designated number of earth books, award them with the certificate below.

Is on Top of the World in Reading

23

Reading Is out of This World!

What on earth is the book about?

_____
_____
_____
_____
_____
_____

When on earth did it happen?

_____
_____
_____
_____
_____
_____

Why on earth?

_____
_____
_____
_____
_____
_____

Where on earth did it happen?

_____
_____
_____
_____
_____
_____

Who on earth are the main characters?

_____
_____
_____
_____
_____
_____
_____

GA1342

Climb to the Top in Reading!

Earth to Student: Each time you read a book from the library, you are recycling. Record the titles and authors on the tree leaves on this page.

Story Starters

Earth to Student: Help finish this story and bring it back to earth. Happy landing!

Once upon a time a _____ landed on planet Earth. When _____

got out of his _____, he looked around and _____

_____

_____

_____

_____

_____

_____

_____

_____

_____

_____

_____

_____

_____

_____

_____

_____

_____

_____

_____

_____

GA1342

The Earth's Treasures

Ahoy there, students! Can you fill this treasure chest with the earth's treasures?

What treasures do you think the earth holds?

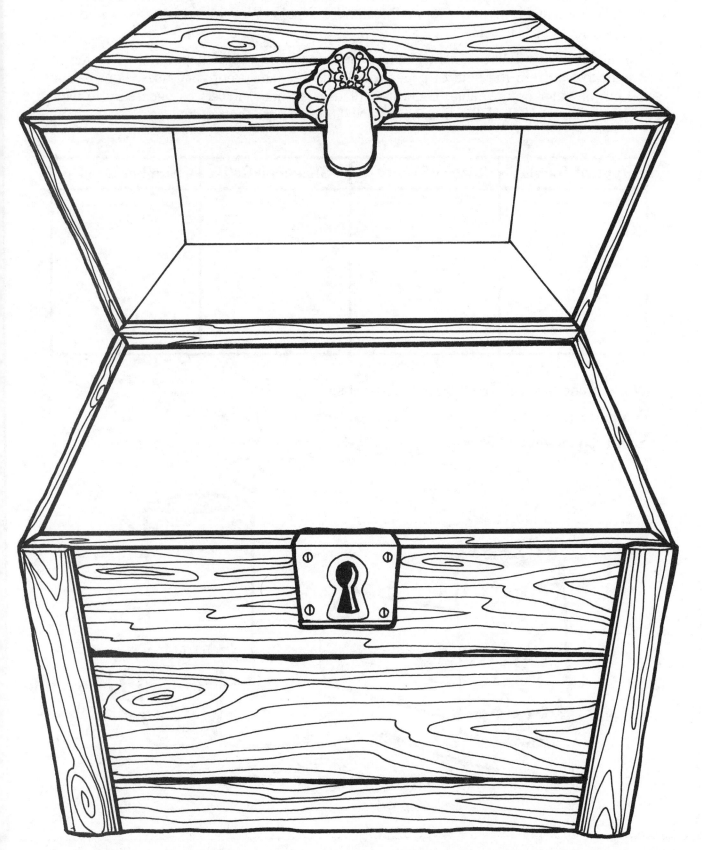

GA1342

Towel Patrol

Earthly Idea: It's better to use cloth towels than paper ones because cloth towels are reusable. But paper towels are convenient and many people like to use them. If your family uses paper towels, do an experiment to discover which brand is the most absorbent. *Absorbent* means how much water the towel will hold. Why would it be better to use an absorbent paper towel?

Earthly Activity: Each student in the class brings in a roll of paper towels or ten to twenty towels from the kind of paper towels his/her family normally uses. Pour ¼ cup (60 ml) of water onto a table. Each student uses as many towels as necessary to wipe up the spill completely. Fill in the chart below and compare the results.

Type of Towels	Size of Sheets	Sheets on Roll	Number Used

Which brand of paper towels was the most absorbent?

Brainstorm: What can you use instead of paper towels at home?

Earth to Homework: Share the results of your experiment with your family.

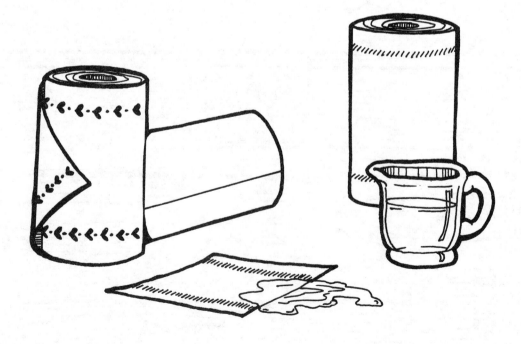

Earth to Homework

Discuss these September earth tips with your family. Can you come up with other ways to save the earth? Draw a picture of your idea or one of the ones below.

- Save gasoline. Join a car pool, ride the school bus, walk, ride a bike whenever you can.

- Instead of using fertilizers for your spring garden, start a compost now. Your homemade fertilizer will be ready by spring.

- Recycle old favorites. Give your old toys to the next generation or trade with friends.

- Be kind to a pet. Put out bird feed or support the zoo. Animals are our earthmates.

- Be a trash collector. Whether you are going on a picnic or a hike, take along a paper bag to collect your trash and the trash that others have left behind.

- Be an energy saver. Wash the laundry with cold water. Air-dry clean dishes.

- Save your aluminum cans for recycling. When the aluminum of the earth is used up, there will be no more.

- Sort the garbage. Recycle. Cut up boxes and separate glass, paper and aluminum. Landfills are filling up so compact your garbage.

- Don't waste water. Don't leave the faucet running while you brush your teeth. Take showers rather than baths.

- Lights out. When you leave a room, always turn off the lights.

GA1342

Follow That Vein

Earthly Activity: Place a leaf between two sheets of thin paper. Rub a crayon across the sheet covering the leaf. Your "rubbing" should show the network of veins that run through a leaf. These veins act as "pipelines" between the leaves and the rest of the tree.

Follow the maze of veins in the leaf below to get to the tree branch.

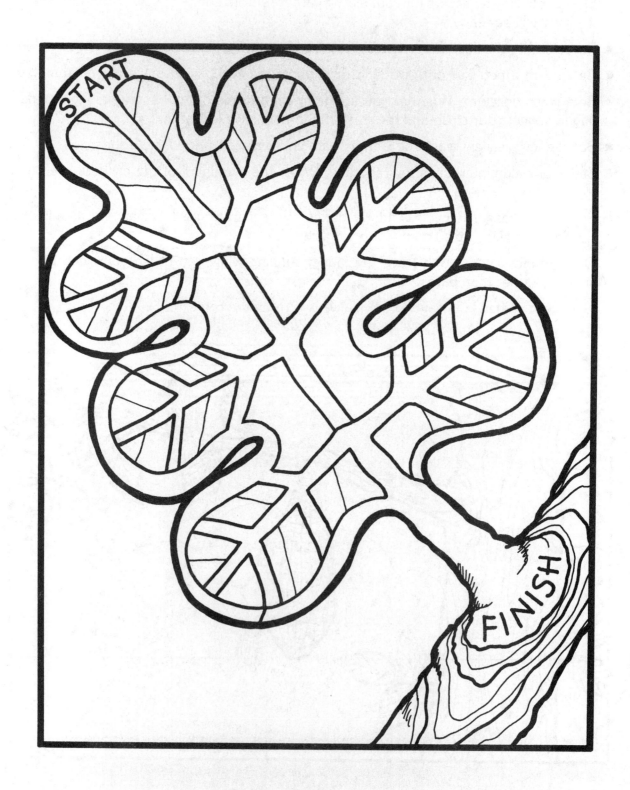

GA1342

Earth Awards

The Greatest Work on Earth Award

is presented to

_____
student

Keep Up the Great Work!

_____
teacher

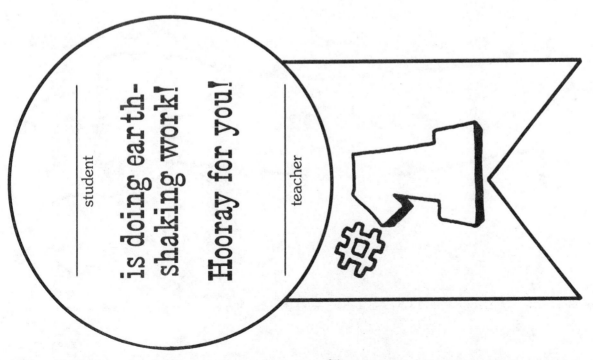

student

is doing earth-shaking work!

Hooray for you!

teacher

GA1342

What on Earth You Can Do in

October

32

GA1342

Earth Words for October

Recycle: To reuse the material in a new way

Precycle: Buying things that come in packages that can be recycled or have already been recycled

Aluminum: A silver-white metallic element that is very lightweight and flexible

Compost: A mixture of dead leaves, decaying organic materials, grass clippings used as fertilizer

Landfill: An area set aside for the disposal of garbage

Disposable: A product designed for temporary use and then to be thrown away

Biodegradable: A substance which will naturally decay and dispose of itself over time

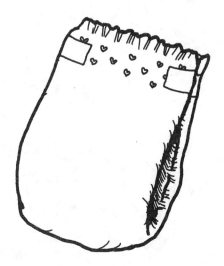

Sort: The process of separating objects into categories

Packaging: The outer wrappings of a product including the box, container or decorative cover

GA1342

Mixed-Up Vocabulary

Earthly Activity: Find an earth word to complete each sentence. Unscramble the earth words and use one to complete each sentence.

naggikcAp _____

Rost _____

nummulA _____

ceceRly _____

flAdlinl _____

girdAledabboe _____

celecpRy _____

stompoc _____

blossIpaed _____

My mother likes to wrap leftovers in _____.

After I cut the grass, I rake the clippings into the _____.

The trashman takes all of our garbage to the _____.

I _____ when I only buy eggs in paper cartons.

Please don't put your aluminum cans in the trash; _____ them.

_____ diapers are designed to be thrown away after using them.

_____ objects will naturally decay over time.

Have you ever been surprised to see how small a toy is when you take it out of its _____?

Get Ready, Set, Recycle Word Search

Search for recyclable items among the letters in the square. Circle each word that you find. *Aluminum foil* is done for you.

X	Y	A	L	U	M	I	N	U	M	A	B	D	R	B	M	Z	K
B	F	O	I	L	X	Q	R	C	A	N	X	Y	B	O	O	K	D
F	I	L	T	E	R	F	G	L	A	S	S	L	H	O	U	S	E
B	D	E	D	I	A	P	E	R	G	E	N	V	E	L	O	P	E
I	N	S	T	R	U	M	E	N	T	H	J	U	N	K	J	L	M
K	I	T	C	H	E	N	D	A	P	P	L	I	A	N	C	E	S
L	O	C	K	A	M	Q	U	I	L	T	R	O	L	L	E	R	O
T	R	S	Q	P	A	P	E	R	P	O	N	S	K	A	T	E	S
T	R	E	E	S	C	J	K	N	O	P	Q	S	C	A	R	F	N
U	Y	G	H	I	H	L	M	J	X	R	A	Y	R	T	V	M	Z
E	A	O	F	F	I	C	E	A	S	U	P	P	L	I	E	S	P
V	R	C	D	F	N	A	B	C	D	L	M	W	A	T	E	R	A
A	N	B	E	N	E	W	S	P	A	P	E	R	A	W	T	R	E
U	N	I	F	O	R	M	V	A	U	L	T	N	Z	I	N	C	O

aluminum foil
book
can
diaper
envelope
filter
glass

house
instrument
junk
kitchen appliances
lock
machine

newspaper
office supplies
paper
quilt
roller skates
scarf
trees

uniform
vault
water
X ray
yarn
zinc

35

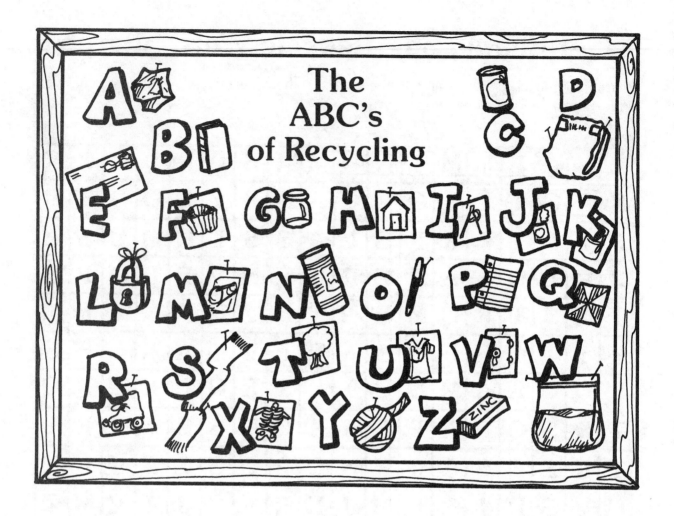

The ABC's of Recycling

Here's a great bulletin board that teaches students about recycling while reinforcing the alpahbet and beginning sounds.

Assign a letter to each child and have him bring in an object or a picture from a magazine that has the same beginning sound. Each can be placed on the board by the appropriate alphabet letter. Students can record their own inventory of objects in a notebook.

A aluminum foil
B book
C can
D diaper
E envelope
F filter
G glass
H house
I instrument
J junk
K kitchen appliances
L lock
M machine

N newspaper
O office supplies
P paper
Q quilt
R roller skate
S scarf
T tree
U uniform
V vault
W water
X X ray
Y yarn
Z zinc

GA1342

Be a Winner with Recycling Bingo

B	I	N	G	O

Play bingo! Have students bring in twenty-five bottle caps, old game pieces or pebbles. Duplicate the bingo card above and give one to each child. On the board have the class list twenty-five recyclable items; then ask each student to randomly fill in the squares on the card with these words. Sample words include *aluminum cans, paper, pie tins, plastic egg cartons, paper bags, jars, clothes,* etc. Simultaneously complete a card in the same manner but cut it into squares. These are the bingo pieces. The first student to complete a row diagonally, vertically or horizontally as the words are called is the winner. Winners win a free pass to the library to "recycle" a story by checking out an old favorite.

GA1342

Scavenger Hunt

Earth to Homework: Here's a fun way to reinforce awareness of threats to the environment and encourage group cooperation. Have students search for items or pictures that could be recycled, are about to become extinct or misuse one of earth's resources. First divide the class into five groups. Give each group a 3″ x 5″ (7.6 x 12.7 cm) card with five items written on them or ask each group to list five items classmates could find at home. Give the class time to divide the tasks.

Some items to find:

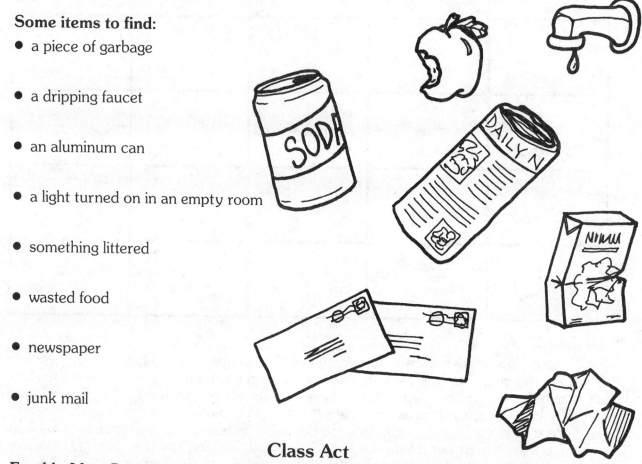

- a piece of garbage

- a dripping faucet

- an aluminum can

- a light turned on in an empty room

- something littered

- wasted food

- newspaper

- junk mail

Class Act

Earthly Idea: Put your class in action with this grand finale. Brainstorm with your class about all the ways they could put their scavenger hunt treasures to use. Reinforce the notion of recycling for the whole school by building a scavenger sculpture that can be placed in the lobby of the school with posters depicting the principles the class has learned.

GA1342

Recycle Concentration

Cut out the cards below. Place them facedown. Student takes a turn by turning over two cards. If they match, he keeps them and tries again. If they don't match, the next player gets a try. Whoever has the most pairs at the end of the game wins.

GA1342

It's in the Bag
in
October

Encourage student awareness of waste output. Have each student decorate a brown paper lunch bag with crayons and markers. Put the bags on the board and challenge students to not fill them.

Earthly Idea: Collect paper grocery bags. Have each student cut out a circle in the bottom of the bag. This will be where the child's head protrudes. Cut armholes in the sides. Have an art activity and let students paint the bags and transform them into Halloween costumes.

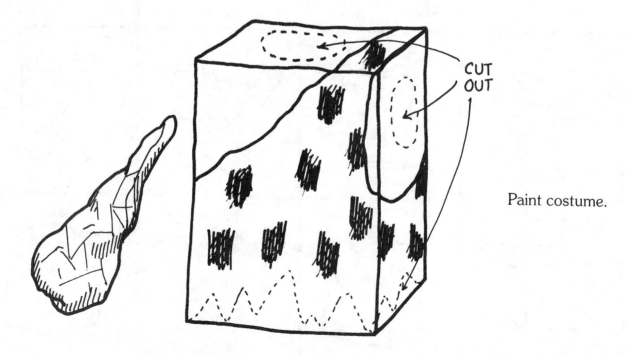

CUT OUT

Paint costume.

40

GA1342

Every "Bunny" Can Recycle!

Here's a great bulletin board to use in April to emphasize recycling. Duplicate a rabbit for each student and add his name. Student could glue a cotton ball on his rabbit each time he recycles.

Recycle This Board: Change the title. No "Bunny" Likes Pollution, No "Bunny" Likes Littering, Every "Bunny" Loves the Earth, Some "Bunny" Loves the Earth, Hop to It and Recycle, We Are All Ears for Saving the Earth

41

GA1342

Get Ready, Set, Recycle!

Design a birdhouse just for fun. Make it energy efficient and high tech! Have fun.

Build a Birdhouse

Use a clean milk carton and make a birdhouse. Fill it with birdseed and help our feathered friends.

1. Ask a grown-up to help cut out two rectangles on opposite sides.

2. Add stickers to the milk carton.

3. Pierce a hole in the carton and add a string to the top for hanging.

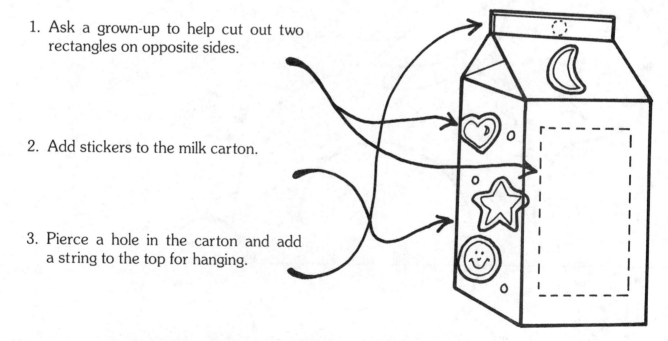

42

GA1342

Cross the Earth Word Puzzle

Across

1. When you watch something carefully, you are an _____.

3. When you throw away trash and recycle it, you must _____ the objects and separate them.

4. We can _____ to save the earth by recycling.

9. The air, water, minerals and all external factors that affect an organism is the _____.

10. The system which evolves among all organisms in an environment is the _____.

Down

2. If you throw chemicals in the ocean, this is called _____.

5. Don't _____. Keep America beautiful!

6. We live on planet _____.

7. My family sorts our trash. Does your family _____?

8. Don't throw away dead leaves and trash. Make them into a _____.

GA1342

October Wonders

This is the perfect bulletin board to emphasize the precious nature of earth's wonders. On one side of the board place wintery pictures of bare trees, bare landscapes and desert-like areas. On the other side post pictures of spring settings and the world in full glory. Read the Greek myth about Persephone to your class.

Ask your students to imagine what the earth would be like if rather than becoming dormant, all of earth's treasures are permanently lost. Using the story starter below or one of the student's own creation, have each student write a story of what it is like to live in a polluted world where spring never comes. Post the students completed stories on the bulletin board.

GA1352

The Grocery Game

Be an earth-conscious shopper. Fill your cart with items that can be recycled. Fill the other cart with products that can't. Happy shopping!

Did you know that when you buy things that come in packages that can be recycled or are made of materials that already have been recycled, this is called precycling?

GA1342

This Board Is Trash!

Use this bulletin board to emphasize how much trash can build up in four weeks. Have students pin their trash to the board each day. Use this display to discuss where trash goes. How does recycling help? How does separating items help? How can we reduce our own trash each day?

46

How Does Man Fill a Landfill?

Here's the perfect bulletin board for encouraging your students to use biodegradable items. From disposable diapers to plastic bags to Styrofoam fast food containers, have students bring in items that can be pinned to the board to illustrate the point.

Brainstorm with your class and discuss ways to counteract the use of these items.

- Students could petition a fast food chain to use only recycled containers.
- Students could write articles about the positive use of cloth diapers.
- Ask students to list creative uses for old containers (i.e. birdhouse from milk carton).
- Challenge students to create gifts from throwaways. What ideas do they come up with?
- Can they think of three uses for each of the following: plastic egg cartons, bottle caps, plastic bags from newspapers?

GA1342

Packaging Pack Up!

Use this bulletin board to demonstrate to students how wasteful and misleading the packages that items come in can be. Before winter vacation ask students to keep the boxes and packages they receive that are overly large, wasteful or misleading. Be sure to send a note to Mom and Dad so they won't mind keeping the *trash*. Add these items, as well as pictures from magazines and catalogues of overwrapped items to the bulletin board.

Earthly Activity: After discussing the problems with overpackaging, have students use the form below to write a letter to a toy company or food packager about how their packaging could be changed to be more efficient and less wasteful or damaging to the environment.

Dear _____,

Here are my ideas about the toys you make and their packages.

_____

_____

_____

_____

_____

_____

_____

_____

_____

_____
(Student's name)

48

Recycling Match

There are many ways to recycle. Can you match each word in column A to a word or idea in column B that will help save the earth's treasures?

Column A **Column B**

GA1342

The ABC's of Recycling

Earth to Student: There are many things that you can recycle. Can you follow the directions and find the items that begin with *A, B, C?*

Circle the items that begin with *A*.

Put an *X* on the top of items that begin with *B*.

Write your name on the top of items that can begin with *C*.

GA1342

Recycled Books Become Best-Sellers!

Books are easily recycled. What books do you enjoy reading or listening to again and again? Perhaps your friends would enjoy reading the book, too. On Recycle Day, bring your favorite books to school to share with your classmates.

Earthly Activity: Select a book you have read recently that you liked. Create an ad campaign for the book. Use the questions below to guide your plan; then create a one-minute commercial for your book.

Why should someone read this book? _____

_____

_____

What makes this book different from others? _____

_____

_____

Who are your favorite characters? _____

_____

_____

What part of this book did you like best? _____

_____

_____

If there is one reason someone should read this book, what is it? _____

_____

_____

What would be a good slogan to describe this book? _____

_____

_____

GA1342

Whoooo Can Recycle?

Aluminum is one of the earth's treasures. When it is all used up there will be no more aluminum on earth. Many cans are made out of steel or tin, but many are made out of aluminum which can be recycled.

Earthly Activities:

- Build a Can Man. Ask students to bring in a selection of clean used cans. Not all cans can be recycled. Make a display of tin cans, steel cans and aluminum cans so students can learn ways to identify them.

- Hold that can! What can be used instead of cans? Have students cut out pictures of can substitutes. As a class project, fill in the chart below.

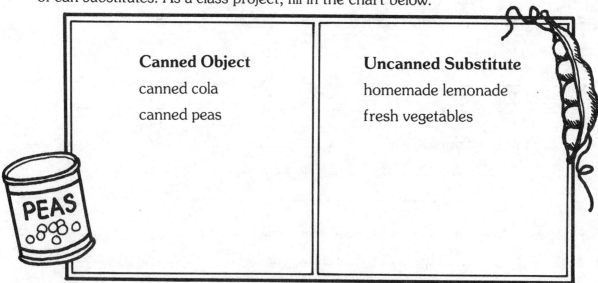

Canned Object	Uncanned Substitute
canned cola	homemade lemonade
canned peas	fresh vegetables

- Save that foil. Have students save cleaned aluminum foil for one month. Use the foil in an art activity during the month of October. Have students shape the foil into spooky Halloween creatures like bats and ghosts. Add the finished products to the bulletin board.

GA1342

Swap and Shop

This bulletin board may also be used in December for exchanging students' toys. Each student can bring in an item under $2 that he or she wants to swap. Add actual items or pictures to the board and let students trade their items for others. Students can choose numbers to see who goes first! Use the activity below to inspire clever ads for each item. Have students circle appealing want ads in the newspaper. What makes these ads inviting?

Toy for Swap

Like new, toy. . . _____

_____

_____

_____

Write your ad in the box above.

GA1342

"Egg"citing Egg Carton Creations!

Be a good egg and recycle egg cartons. Here are some "egg"citing ideas!

Egg Carton Alphabet: Write letters of the alphabet inside the carton (two letters per space). Place four pebbles or coins in the egg carton. Close it up and shake it. Open it up and record the letters. See how many words you can make after taking five turns.

Creepy Crawlers: Cut one row of a paper egg carton. Paint it with tempera paint. Add eyes, antennas and details to make a creepy crawler.

Super Glasses: Add pipe cleaners to two sections cut from a cardboard egg carton. Cut holes and decorate.

Junk to Jewels: Decorate a cardboard egg carton with odds and ends and personalize it with your name or a friend's. This is a great box for holding junk or jewels.

GA1342

Make a Time Bottle

Earth to Student: Even though it sounds like fun, never send up a message in a helium balloon or across the sea in a bottle. The balloon might be mistaken as food by a bird, or when it deflates a fish might eat it. Besides, the balloon and bottle are other pollutants in our air and in the sea.

Earthly Activity: Now for fun, here's your chance to send your message to the world in a safe time bottle. What message do you want to send to the world in your bottle? You can use the bottle below to send your message across the room. After every student puts a message in the bottle, pass the sheets around the room, letting the students read each other's. On the board categorize the messages and talk about the students' concerns for the future.

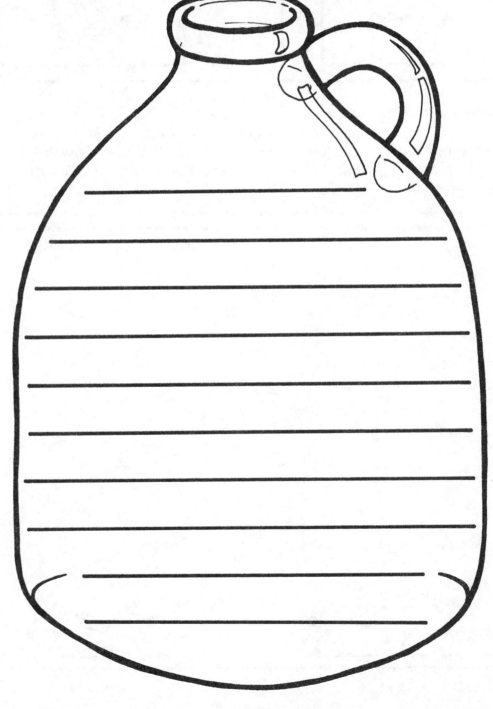

GA1342

Litterers Are Losers!

Litterbugs Unite!

Let Up on Litter!

Earthly Activity: Now that you are a concerned, aware citizen, you must inform others. Create a slogan to stop littering. What makes a slogan effective? It should be brief, clear and to the point. Use the area below to sketch your ideas for a poster with your slogan. Hang up your posters throughout the school. Ask store owners in the neighborhood to hang up the posters.

Oh, Boy—It's a Toy

Earth to Student: Here's a list to help you inventory your toys. Don't throw away used or broken ones. Find ways to recycle them. List the toys you can hand down or give away, the ones you can repair and new ways to use old toys.

Give It Away	Fix It	Recycle It
Example: Give game to cousin Ed	Glue leg on doll	Save dice and paper money for another game.
1. _____	_____	_____
2. _____	_____	_____
3. _____	_____	_____
4. _____	_____	_____
5. _____	_____	_____
6. _____	_____	_____
7. _____	_____	_____
8. _____	_____	_____

GIVE TO ANN

RECYCLE

FIX

GA1342

Make Glass Last!

Earth to Student: Glass can be recycled at factories, and with your help we can save energy by recycling it at home. Clean out the bottles and take off the caps. Sort the bottles in boxes that are reusable and every week take them to the recycling center. Sort the glass by color—clear, green and brown. Each time you recycle glass at home, have your family add a check (or draw the bottle) in the box.

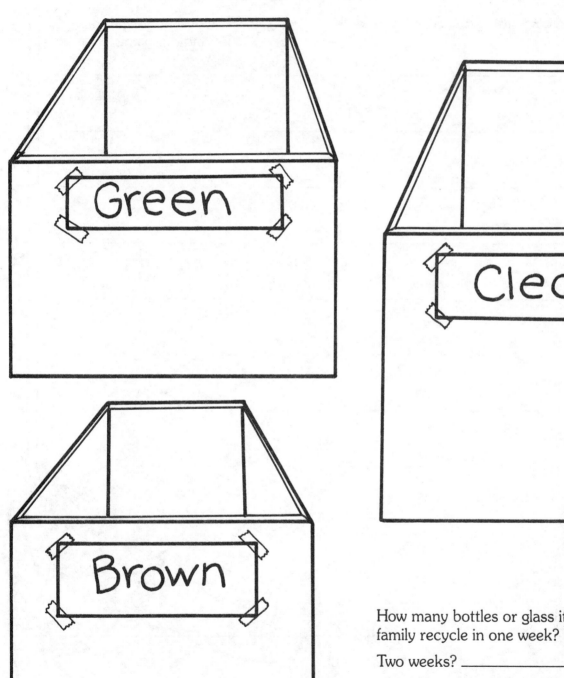

How many bottles or glass items did your family recycle in one week? _____

Two weeks? _____

Three weeks? _____

GA1342

Art's My Bag

Earthly Projects: Here are some fun art projects for recycling bags and sacks.

Potato Sacks

1. Cut squares from potato sacks and tape the edges.

2. Use yarn to weave in and out, over and under to make a design. This weaving should alternate rows by starting under on one row, over on the next.

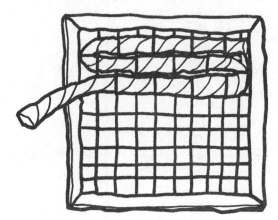

Trash Bash

1. Take a wad of paper and instead of throwing it away, toss it into bags.

2. Number each bag and see how many points you can score with a piece of trash.

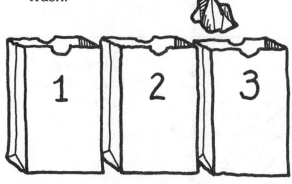

Turkey Bags

1. Stuff half of a lunch bag with newspaper.

2. Pinch it closed at the half point and tie or tape the gather to stay in place. Leave extra paper for the tail.

3. Cut out a head and feathers and add them to the bag.

FOLD AND PASTE

Enlarge pattern.

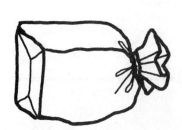

GA1342

Have a Bash with Trash

Earth to Student: Help mash trash and reduce landfills. Fill in the answers here and have a bash with trash.

What is trash?	Where does it come from?	Where does it go?
What happens to the trash?		**How can you help reduce trash?**

60

GA1342

October Trick or "Tree"ts

Here's a fun bulletin board to use in October. See if you can trick your students by stumping them with the wrong answers. Duplicate twenty-four trees, using the patterns below. Write problems on the treetops and sums on the trunks. Mix up the sums. Challenge each student to carefully pin the right trunks to their matching problems. Let each student time himself and try to break his own record.

You can recycle this board by turning over the tree patterns and writing new math problems on each. Try subtraction, multiplication and division, too!

61

GA1342

Every Day Is Earth Day!

Use this bulletin board to encourage students to do good things for the planet Earth, in this case recycling small objects that would otherwise be trash. Duplicate a birthday cake pattern from below for each student and add his name. Hang a small paper bag labeled with each student's name on the board.

Begin a classroom recycling campaign. Ask students to bring in small items that are no longer usable for their original use like bottle caps, screws, old buttons, small seashells and old keys. For every ten items a child puts in his bag, he may have one candle on his cake. Encourage the children to count by ten's when they describe how many items they have recycled.

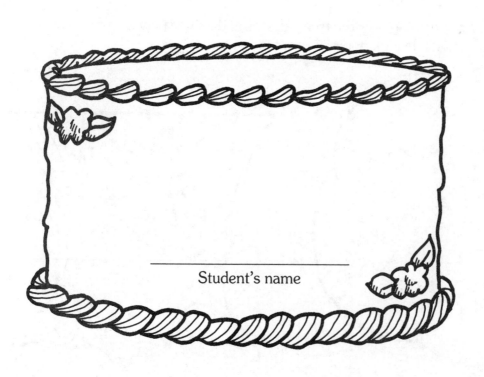

Student's name

62

GA1342

The Name Game

Earthly Ideas: All the activities recycle a child's name in new ways. Try your own John Hancock for fun.

Letter Up: How many earth words can you make from the letters in your name?

Example: Robert

Name Plaques: Using recyclable objects like bottle caps, buttons, yarn, comic cutouts and magazines, make a name plaque for yourself.

Magazine Search: Give a new use to an old magazine. Have students search for pictures of things that begin with each letter of their names.

Earthly Game: What's on Earth?
How many things on earth can you find using the letters in the word *earth*?

E is for elephant . . .
A is for aluminum cans . . .
R is for rain . . .
T is for trees . . .
H is for home . . .

GA1342

Earth Awards

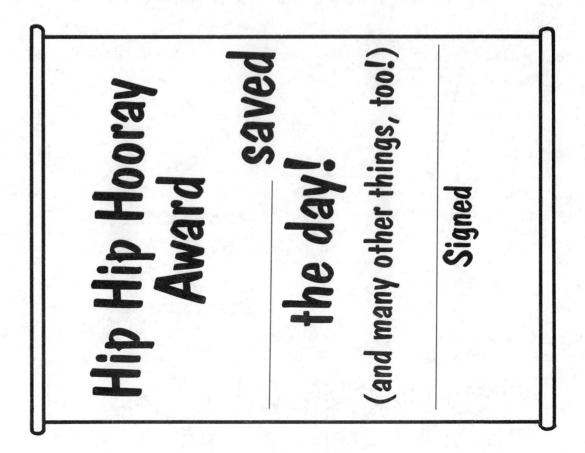

Hip Hip Hooray Award

_____ saved the day!

(and many other things, too!)

_____
Signed

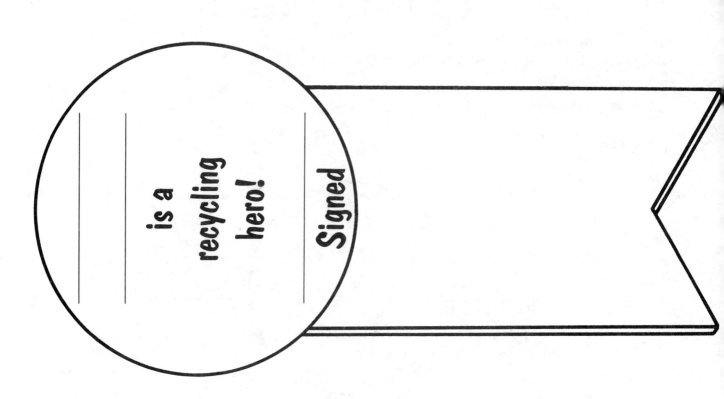

_____ is a recycling hero!

_____
Signed

64

GA1342

What on Earth You Can Do in

November

Nature: The world surrounding man

Ecosystem: A scientific term for all living and nonliving things in the environment and the relationships among them

Food Chain: A series of organisms that are interrelated in their feeding habits so that the smallest is eaten by the next smallest, the next smallest is eaten by the next one in size, etc.

Organism: Any kind of plant or animal life

Phytoplankton: The very tiniest plant life

Zooplankton: The tiniest animal life in the ocean

Community: A group of animals and plants that live together in the same environment

Population: A population is the group of organisms that live in the same area all the time.

Predators: Animals that eat other animals

GA1342

Decode and Discover

Earthly Activity: Use the code to discover the words below.

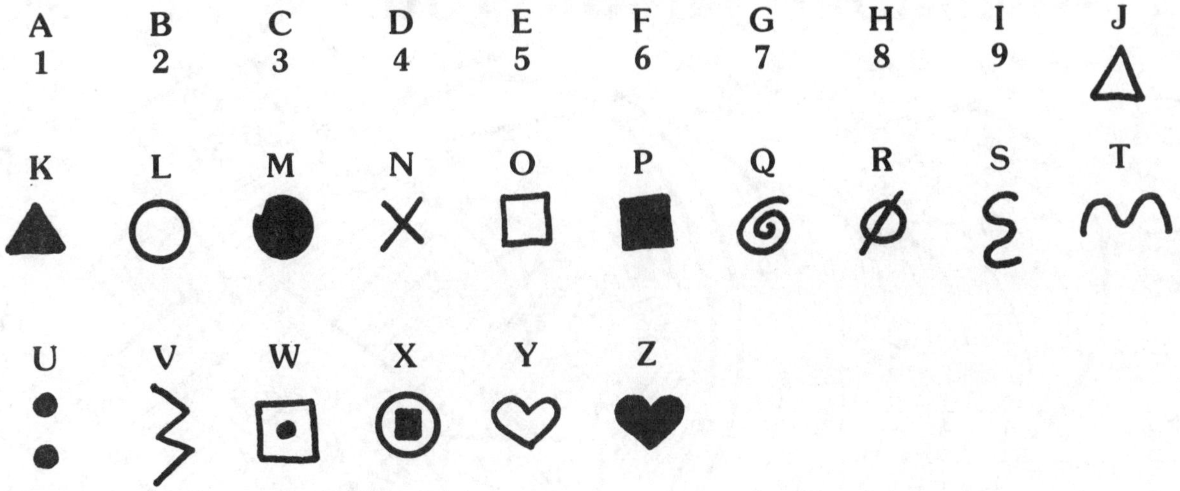

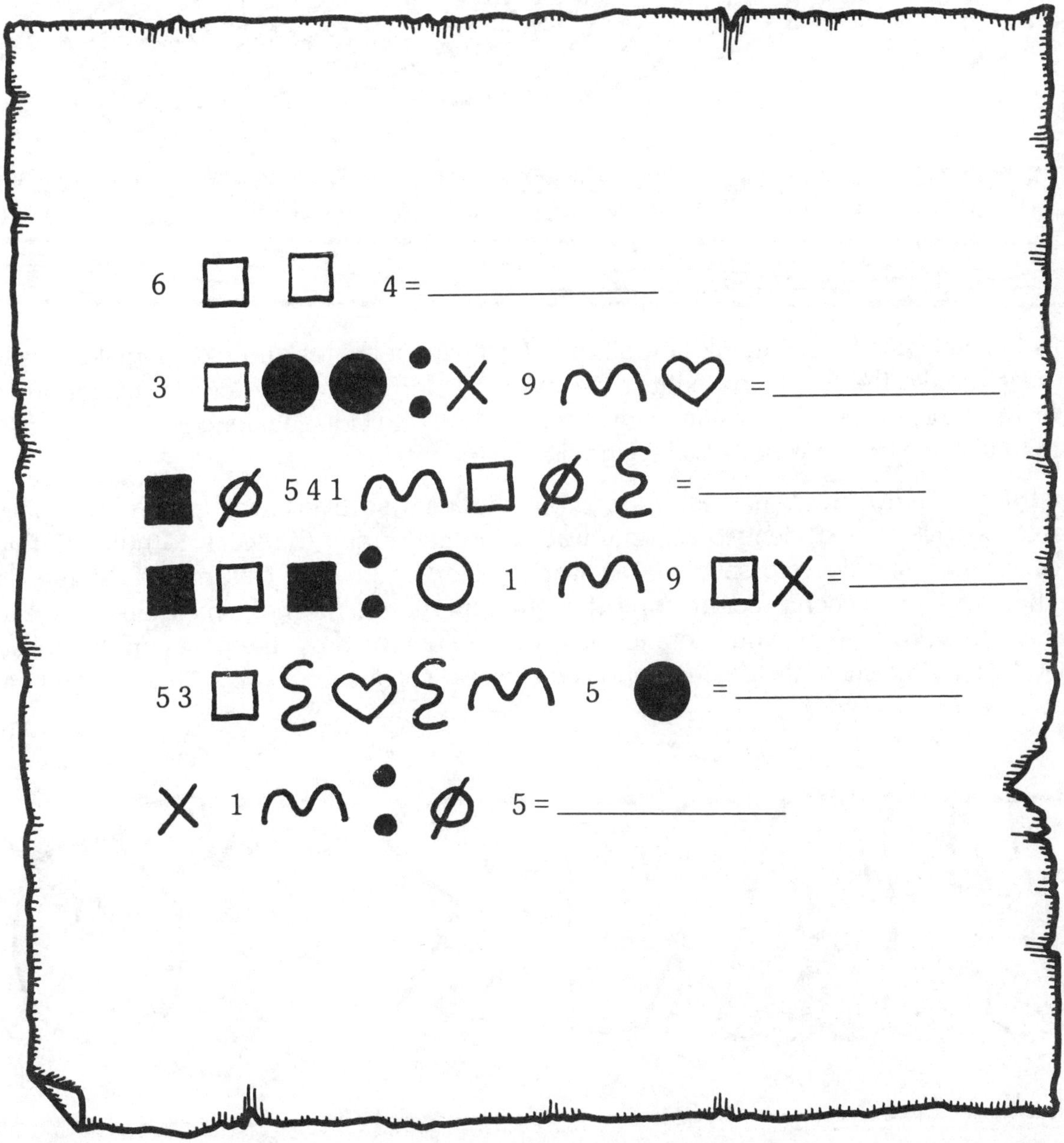

A	B	C	D	E	F	G	H	I	J
1	2	3	4	5	6	7	8	9	△

K	L	M	N	O	P	Q	R	S	T
▲	○	●	X	□	■	ⵔ	ø	Ɛ	ʍ

U	V	W	X	Y	Z
⠒	⋗	⊡	⊙	♡	♥

6 □ □ 4 = _____

3 □ ● ● ⠒ X 9 ʍ ♡ = _____

■ ø 5 4 1 ʍ □ ø Ɛ = _____

■ □ ■ ⠒ ○ 1 ʍ 9 □ X = _____

5 3 □ Ɛ ♡ Ɛ ʍ 5 ● = _____

X 1 ʍ ⠒ ø 5 = _____

GA1342

November Thank-You's

This bulletin board gives thanks for all the efforts schoolmates and others make to save the earth. Use the thank-you pattern below to border the bulletin board. Decorate the board with headlines, pictures and news stories about individuals taking care of the earth. Add to your collection with items brought in by students.

Earthly Activity: Swap names among your students so everyone has a secret pal in the class. Tell each student to secretly watch the pal during the week to note anything special he or she does to save the environment or be kind to classmates. At the end of the week have each student copy the "stationery" on the next page and ask each student to write a "thank-you" note to the observed person. Post the notes on the bulletin board asking the students to guess who is the secret pal in each.

GA1342

November Salutes You

Dear _____ :

_____

_____

_____

_____

_____

_____

_____

_____

_____

_____

_____

_____

_____

_____

_____

_____

Your admirer,

_____

GA1342

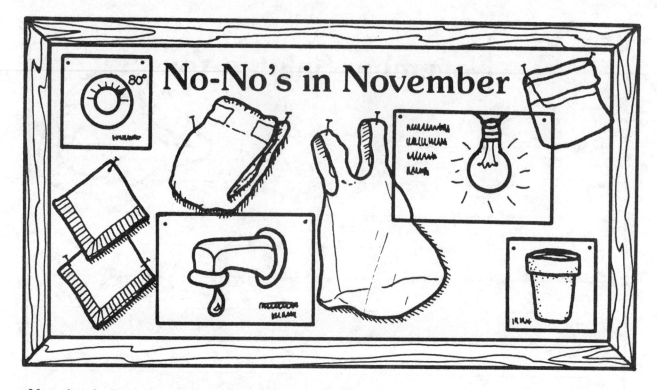

No-No's in November

Use this bulletin board to reinforce things that hurt the earth and open a discussion of opposites. From being wasteful to pollution to littering, etc., students can illustrate their ideas, cut pictures from magazines or write ideas on index cards. Add new ideas daily to collect a multitude of no-no's.

Earthly Activity:

What are antonyms? Does every word have an antonym?

What are the antonyms for these words?

day _____   asleep _____

hot _____   dry _____

fast _____   concentrate _____

Every action has an opposite, too. What are the opposite actions for each no-no below?

No-No's	Yes-Yes's
Using paper diapers	_____
Leaving the lights on when no one is around	_____
Using paper plates	_____
Using plastic grocery bags	_____
Driving everywhere	_____

GA1342

Earth to Student: Election day is the first Tuesday in November. Pretend you are running for class president or better yet, Captain Earth! Tell your voters why they should vote for you. How will you help the earth during your term?

Write your campaign speech here.

VOTE

I will . . .

Elect

GA1342

Helping Hands
for Mother Earth

Brainstorm with your class on how you can lend a hand and help take care of the earth. Duplicate a hand for each student and have him write his ideas on it and add them to the board.

72

First Day on Earth

Earth to Student: How old are you? How old is the earth? The earth has been around for millions of years. In comparison, you have been on earth for only a little while. Pretend it's your birthday—your very first day on earth.

Interview your family and fill out this work sheet. Ask a member of your family to help you look up *earth* in an encyclopedia. Can you learn one new fact about the earth and several new facts about your first day on earth?

My first day on earth was _____

_____.

It was a _____.
                                    (weekday)

The weather on the day I was born was

_____

I was born in _____ on earth.

I was _____ inches (centimeters) tall and

weighed _____ pounds (grams).

The earth is _____ miles
(kilometers) around.

My first day on earth the following things happened or were popular:

Famous event in history _____

Famous birthdays _____

Popular song _____

Popular actor _____

Popular actress _____

Popular movie _____

Popular foods _____

Today we have _____,

but on my first day on earth there were no _____

_____

GA1342

Stand Back

Earthly Idea: To understand the ecosystem, you must take a good look at the world around you. Sometimes we think we understand something, but we are only looking at part of the picture.

Earthly Activity: Look at the illustration below. What is it? It is something you see every day.

- Draw a 1″ (2.54 cm) square on the palm of your hand. Look at the lines inside the square. Do they look similar to the illustration? It would have been easy to identify the drawing if we had included the rest of the picture.

  Sometimes when we look at nature we see only part of the picture. The ecosystem describes the relationship between all the parts of the picture. Your palm is part of your hand that is part of your arm that is part of your body which composes a human being who is one person in a classroom of students in a school of students that is part of a community in a city which is part of a country on the earth that is one planet in the solar system that is part of a galaxy . . . . See how complicated it is?

- Walk outside. Walk up so close to a tree that your nose almost touches the bark. What do you see? Answer the questions below to explain how a tree is part of an ecosystem.

  When you look at the bark, what do you see? _____

  Take three steps back. What kind of tree are you looking at? _____

  Where is the tree? _____

  Where is the school yard? _____

  In what city do you live? _____

GA1342

My Family

Earthly Idea: In some ways a family is like an ecosystem. The members of a family are independent. They need substances in the environment to survive. Some family members are responsible for supplying the needs of other family members. Some family members are dependent on other family members to supply them with food, clothing and shelter.

Earthly Activity: Draw a picture of the members of your family. Who is responsible for taking care of the needs of the family members? Who is more dependent on other family members for survival?

GA1342

My Community

Earthly Activity: To help the students understand the interrelationship of members and parts of a community, have your class create an old-fashioned community. On a large table or area of the floor draw a "Main Street." Divide the class into three groups:

Residential Planners

Commercial Planners

Recreational Planners

Each group is given the charge of planning their particular area of the community.

Some important questions for the class to consider:

Must the groups communicate with each other?

Are there certain areas of the community that should be given particular purposes?

Is the community self-sufficient? Can a resident fill all his basic needs for food, shelter, clothing within the borders of this community? Is that enough for a happy life?

76

GA1342

How Many Are There?

A population is a group of organisms that live in the same place all the time. The word *population* can be used to describe individuals that work, play or live together. It can also describe numbers of other kinds of living things.

Earthly Activity: Answer the following questions:

What is the population of students in your classroom? _____

What is the population of trees on the playground? _____

What is the population of people in your household? _____

What is the population of students in your school? _____

What is the population of the city in which you live? _____

Can you complete the chart below?

City	Population
New York City	_____
Atlanta	_____
Los Angeles	_____
Indianapolis	_____
Chicago	_____
Dallas	_____
Birmingham	_____
Cincinnati	_____

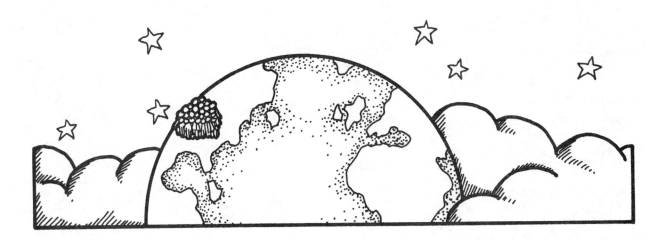

GA1342

The Ecosystem

Earthly Idea: An *ecosystem* is a scientist's term for all the living and nonliving things in an environment and the relationships between them. Introduce the idea of inter-relationships with the matching game below. Have students draw a line between the objects that go together.

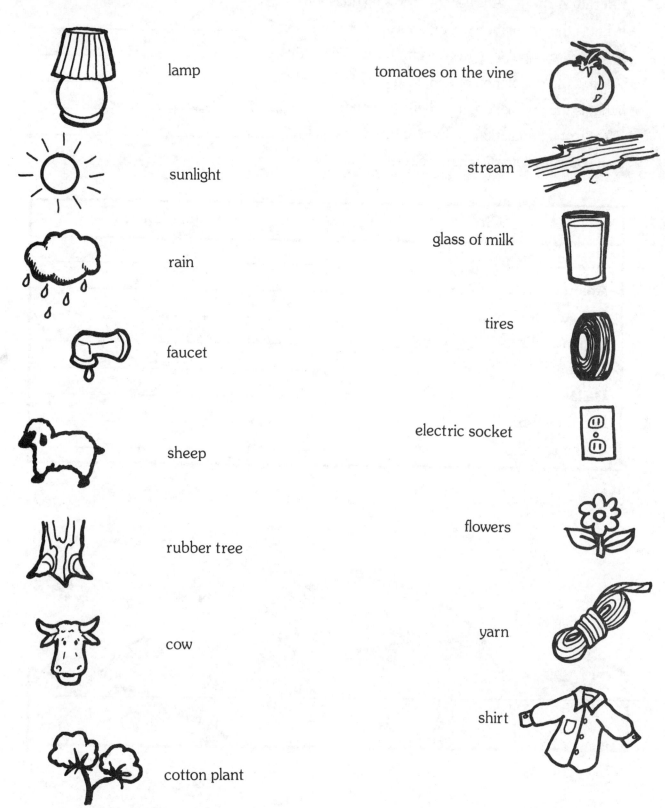

lamp

sunlight

rain

faucet

sheep

rubber tree

cow

cotton plant

tomatoes on the vine

stream

glass of milk

tires

electric socket

flowers

yarn

shirt

GA1342

All Eyes on Earth

Earthly Project: You and scientists have a lot in common. You both must be good observers, ask questions and make conclusions. Pick a category you want to study from the list below. Each day spend fifteen minutes observing the animal, place in the environment or object you have chosen. Collect facts or samples and record your information here. Use the questions below to guide your study.

Tip-Top Topics: birds, rocks, trees, leaves, seeds and nuts, plants, debris, mud sediment, dirt

GA1342

The Balance of Nature

Earthly Idea: Introduce the concept of balance. Have all the students stand up. Have a contest to see who can stand on one foot the longest?

Why did children lose their balance?

What was the longest time someone could stand on one foot?

What interfered with the child's balance?

Earthly Activity: Have each pair of students make a balance scale using string, a ruler and two paper cups.

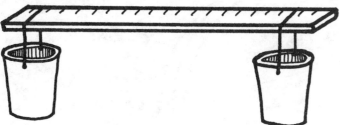

Cut two small holes on opposite sides under the lips of the two paper cups. Cut two 1 foot (.30 m) long pieces of string. Tie the string through the holes in the paper cup so that the string can straddle the ends of the ruler. Place a finger on the center of the ruler so that it balances on the finger. One partner should fill the two cups with the materials below until the scale balances. Then follow the directions in parenthesis and answer the question.

paper clips and seven bottle caps
(Take away three bottle caps.)

What happened? _____

four pieces of chalk and bottle caps
(Take away all but one bottle cap.)

What happened? _____

Use the record sheet on the next page for your observations.

There is a balance in nature, too. That means there is little change from day to day between the numbers of types of plants, animals and other objects in the ecosystem. Sometimes something happens that upsets the balance of nature. A drought may kill all of a particular kind of crop. A disease may kill a particular kind of fish. When one part of the system is changed, it affects another part of the ecosystem.

GA1342

What Makes the Scale Balance?

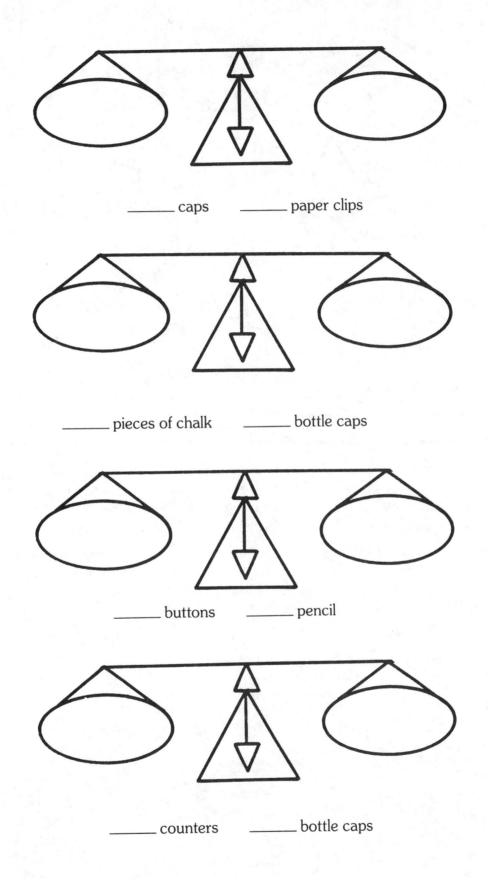

_____ caps   _____ paper clips

_____ pieces of chalk   _____ bottle caps

_____ buttons   _____ pencil

_____ counters   _____ bottle caps

GA1342

The sounds of nature are wonderful to listen to. Your students will love tuning into the sounds they hear as they listen to nature. Take your class on a nature walk. What sounds do they hear? Who or what makes them? Have students illustrate the sounds by drawing who makes them and also collecting pictures to add to the bulletin board.

Brainstorm: Have a class discussion and compare sounds of nature to musical instruments. How do the wind instruments relate? What instrument sounds like a bee buzzing, a woodpecker pecking or a bird singing? Students can design their own instruments and band using Mother Nature's band. Refer to the activity work sheet on the next page and duplicate one for each student.

GA1342

Mother Nature's Band

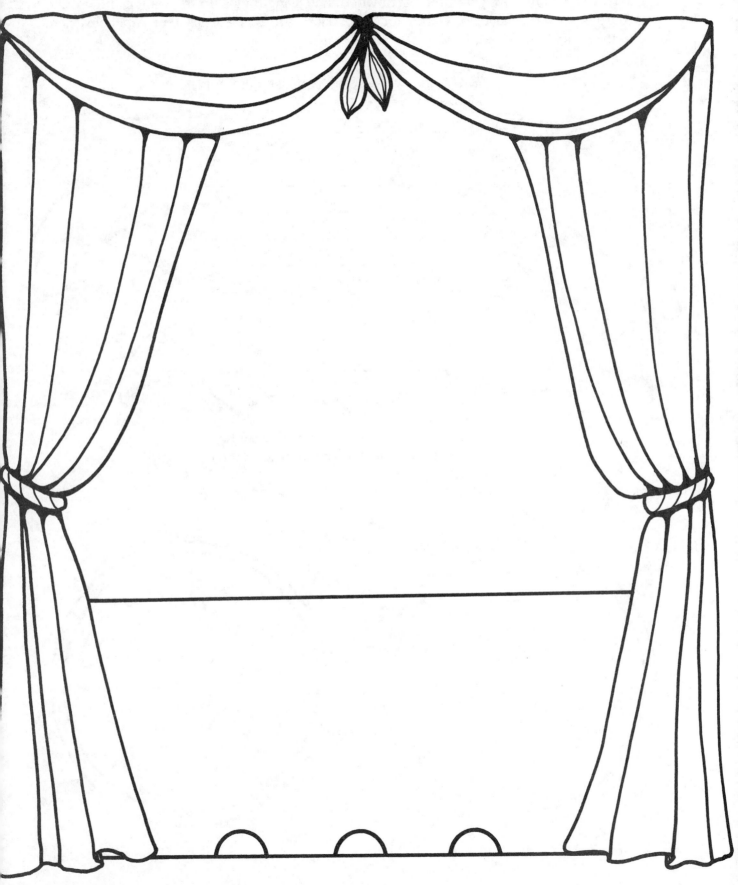

83

GA1342

Bird's the Word Work Sheet

Earth to Student: We share the earth with many living things. In the winter, the ground is harder so birds have to search for food. Here are some ways you can help them and things to learn about.

Bird's the word. Can you list different kinds of birds?

1. _____
2. _____
3. _____
4. _____
5. _____
6. _____
7. _____
8. _____
9. _____
10. _____

Bird watch. Observe birds and draw two different kinds in the binoculars. Happy watching.

What do birds do?   Where do birds live?   What is your state bird?

84

GA1342

Adopt a Spot

Earth to Student: The earth is living and changing constantly. Some man-made changes are not wanted. What kinds of changes take place?

Earthly Activity: Find a spot on earth to adopt for two weeks. Measure an area 4 feet x 4 feet (1.21 x 1.21 m). Collect four sticks to use as stakes at the four corners of the area. Wrap a string around each stake to form a boundary for your spot.

Observe your spot for two weeks. Record your observations by answering these questions.

On the first day how does your spot look? Is it clean, polluted, bare?	How did your spot change over the two weeks?
_____	_____
_____	_____
_____	_____
_____	_____
_____	_____
Did rain change your spot?	**Did people or animals change your spot?**
_____	_____
_____	_____
_____	_____
_____	_____
_____	_____
Do animals live on your spot?	**What other changes did you see?**
_____	_____
_____	_____
_____	_____
_____	_____

GA1342

The Best Little Food Chain on Earth

All animals on earth need food. Plants need energy, too. The sun's energy travels to plants. Plants use sunlight and carbon dioxide and water to produce their own food. The process is called *photosynthesis*.

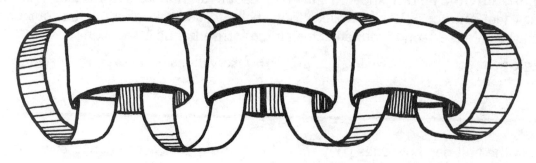

Plant-eating animals eat the plants. Animal-eating animals eat the plant-eating animals.

Can you think of some animals that eat only plants? _____

_____

Can you think of some animals that eat other animals? _____

_____

Earthly Activity: To help you understand the food chain, make a paper chain using colored paper strips that are ½" x 3" (1.25 x 7.62 cm). Form one circle, overlap the ends and glue together. Make next loop but run it through the previous circle; then glue the ends. Cut out the pictures of the plant and animals below. Hang each from a chain in order in the food chain.

Grass

Cow

Lion

Coyote

The Food Chain in the Ocean

Earthly Idea: There is a food chain in the ocean just like there is on earth. Some of the names of the things eaten will be new to you.

Algae uses energy from the sun to grow on the earth's surface. Algae is the green and black growth on rocks in an aquarium. The tiny plants are called *phytoplankton*. These tiny plants are eaten by tiny animals in the ocean called *zooplankton*. Baby fish, baby sea urchins and baby snails are zooplankton.

Earth to Homework: Ask Mom or Dad to take you to a grocery store that has a fish market or go to a bait store. Look at the kinds of fish displayed. In the space below, draw a picture of the smallest fish you see. Draw a picture of the largest fish. What are the names of other fish you see?

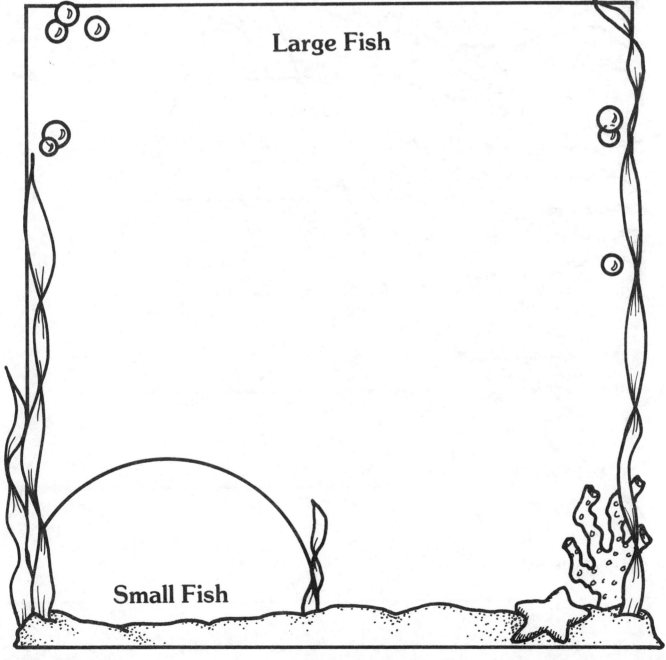

Large Fish

Small Fish

GA1342

The Food Pyramid

Earthly Idea: How many pieces of popcorn can you eat in one sitting? How many ice-cream sundaes could you eat at one meal? The bigger the treat the fewer you can eat.

The food chain is like that too. It is a pyramid because it takes many more animals to satisfy the first part of the chain than it does later. For example, it may take 100,000 phytoplankton to feed 10,000 zooplankton. It may take 10,000 zooplankton to feed 1000 anchovies and 1000 anchovies to feed 100 mackerel and 100 mackerel to feed 10 sea lions and 10 sea lions to feed 1 great white shark.

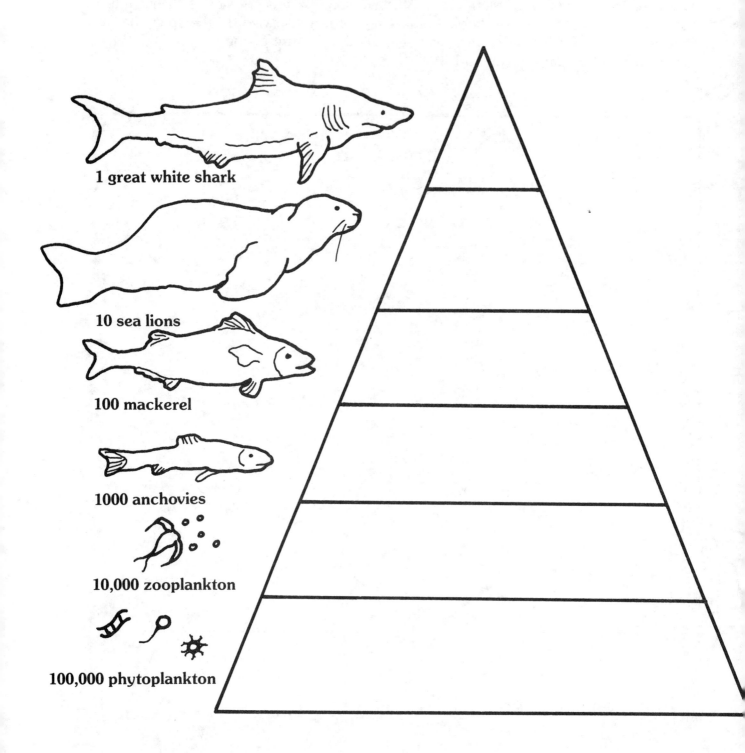

1 great white shark

10 sea lions

100 mackerel

1000 anchovies

10,000 zooplankton

100,000 phytoplankton

GA1342

Fish Chains

Earthly Idea: Just like some animals eat other animals, some fish eat other fish. That too is part of the food chain. Anchovies are small fish that like to eat zooplankton, the tiniest animals in the ocean. Mackerel love to eat anchovies. Sea lions dive into the ocean looking for schools of mackerel. Sharks eat large fish.

Earth to Homework: Cut out the fish in the picture below and paste them on a sheet of paper in a food chain. Which fish would eat which fish? How does size play a role in what eats what?

GA1342

There Are a Lot of Fish in the Sea.
Can You Read These Numbers?

one hundred thousand   ten   one   one billion

one million   one hundred   ten thousand   one thousand

one hundred million   ten million

Write the words for these numbers. Use the words above to help you.

1 anchovy _____

10 anchovies _____

100 anchovies _____

1000 anchovies _____

10,000 anchovies _____

100,000 anchovies _____

1,000,000 anchovies _____

10,000,000 anchovies _____

100,000,000 anchovies _____

1,000,000,000 anchovies _____

Have you ever eaten anchovies on your pizza? How many anchovies do you like to eat?

_____

GA1342

**Good Manner's
Bring You Down to Earth**

Emphasize good manners with this bulletin board. Cut a 24" (.60 m) piece of yarn and attach it to planet Earth. Duplicate a super kid for each of your students and have him decorate it and add his name. Each piece of yarn should be connected to a pattern. Whenever a student exhibits good manners, is polite or helps another student, move his character 2" (5.08 cm) closer to the earth. The goal is to reach the earth and when necessary head back out to outer space. Encourage students to go for it and defy the limits!

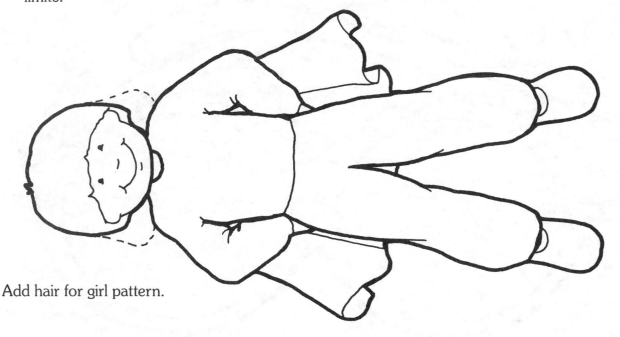

Add hair for girl pattern.

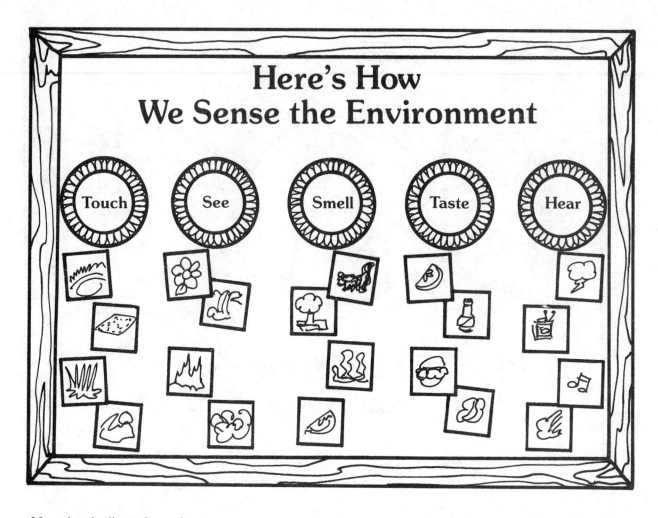

Here's How
We Sense the Environment

Touch   See   Smell   Taste   Hear

Use this bulletin board to encourage your students to use their five senses to experience the environment. Duplicate the work sheet on the next page and instruct students to recycle magazines and search for pictures and illustrations of the items they list. Add them to the bulletin board. Write the five senses on paper plates and categorize the pictures. Duplicate the sunglasses below and give each student one to draw or write sensible ideas for helping the environment.

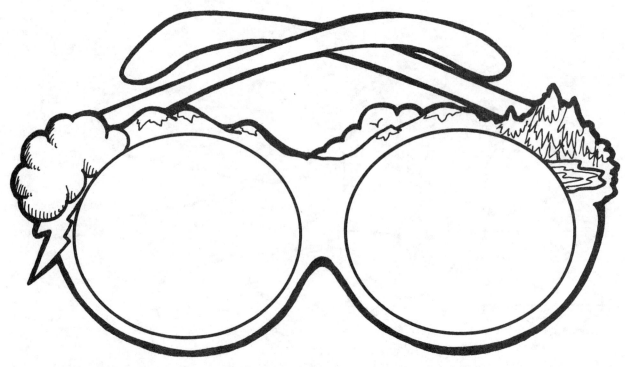

Have a Down-to-Earth Thanksgiving

Write what you are thankful for that is related to the earth.

I am thankful that

I am . . .

I am . . .

I am . . .

I am . . .

Earth

93

GA1342

Don't Let Bugs Bug You!

You don't have to like bugs, but they help the earth, too. Here are some bug facts.

Fireflies help brighten summer nights.

Without insects as pollinators, many plants and food crops could not reproduce.

Worms help make soil rich as they eat their way through the soil. Plants love rich soil, and we need plants.

Bees help spread pollen to other plants. They help the plants grow.

Many insect-eating songbirds, reptiles and amphibians would vanish.

Game fish like trout would have a harder time surviving since they depend on insects for food.

94

What Bugs You?

Earth to Student: What things bother you about the environment? Write a story about the things that bug you and how you would change them.

95

GA1342

What's in a Prefix?

A prefix is a word part that is added to the beginning of a word and changes its meaning. Look at the pairs of words below.

compose	decompose
cycle	recycle
cycle	precycle

Circle the word part that has been added to each of the words in the second column. *De-*, *re-* and *pre-* are prefixes. How do they change the meaning of each word?

Add the prefix to each word below to make a new word.

re + do = redo

re + make = _____

re + hire = _____

pre + packaged = _____

pre + set = _____

Can you find the prefixes in the words below? Underline each prefix in the list of words below. How does it change the meaning of the word?

supermarket

superman

renew

unhappy

unlike

reusable

unclean

nonbiodegradable

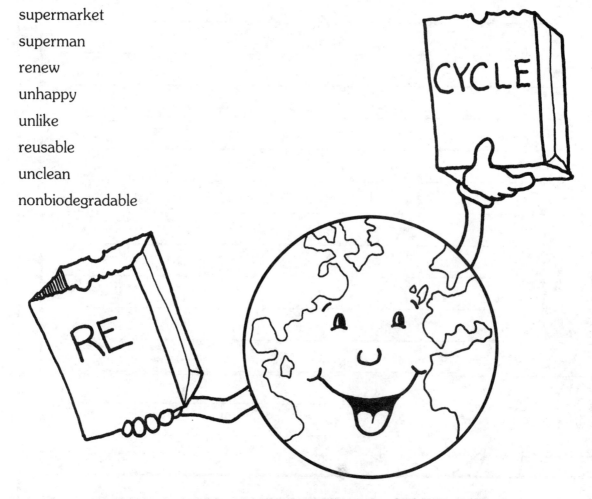

GA1342

Earth Award

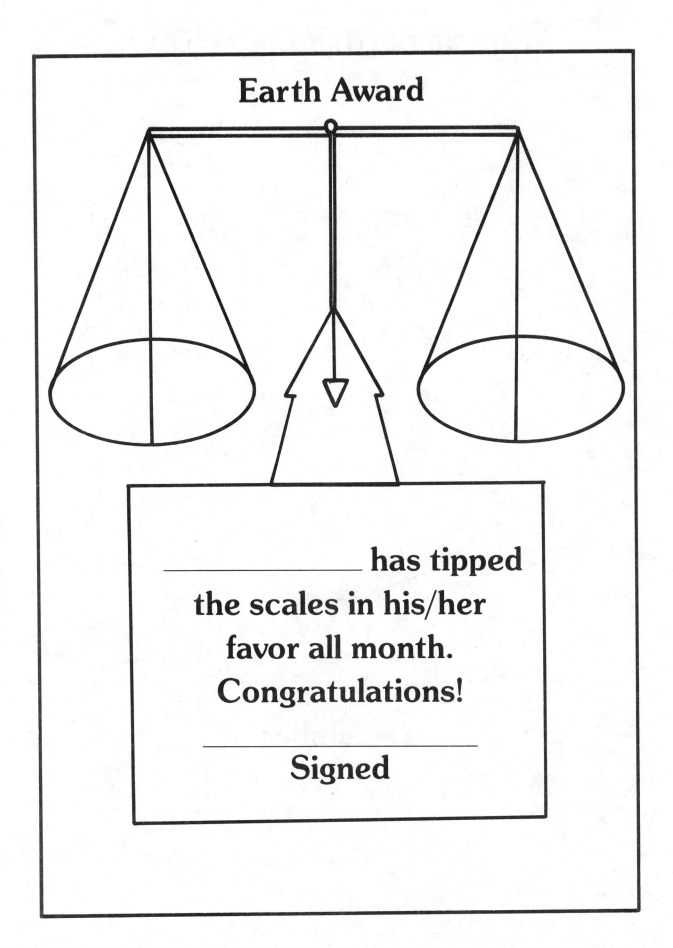

_____ has tipped the scales in his/her favor all month. Congratulations!

_____
Signed

97

What on Earth You Can Do in

December

Earth Words for

December

Pollution: The after effect of making something dirty or foul, whether it is air pollution or water pollution

Junk Mail: Any letter or object that arrives through the mail which is unwanted, unsolicited or unnecessary

Slogan: A distinctive phrase which calls to mind a particular idea

Litter: Trash which is not disposed of properly so it mars property

Coupon: A certificate or ticket that entitles the holder to a discount or some other benefit

Occupant: Someone living in a space

Decibel: The term used to measure the loudness of a sound

Greenhouse Effect: The term used to describe an atmospheric condition that contributes to warmer average temperatures on earth

---

Draw a line from the picture to the word that best describes the picture.

litter

coupon

occupant

air pollution

junk mail

The Wonderful World of Words

How many words can you make from the letters in the following words. If a letter appears twice, you can use it twice, but if a letter appears once, then it can be used only one time.

pollution	littering	recycle

environment	endangered	solution

Earthly Activity: Prefixes change the meanings of words. Look at the two words below.

Pollution **Antipollution**

Suffixes also change the meanings of words or the way they may be used in sentences. The suffix *-tion* is added to each word below. Use the old word and the new word in a sentence.

pollute	
pollution	
collect	
collection	
conserve	
conservation	
transport	
transportation	
produce	
production	

How does *-tion* change the meaning or use of the word?

GA1342

Car Pools Save Gas!
Fewer Cars/Less Pollution

How many car pools are there in your class? How many children are there in your class? If each person in your school was driven to school by a parent, how many more cars would drive to your school each day?

Earthly Activity: The exhaust from your car contributes to air pollution. Put your best foot forward and walk more often. Ask your parent to acompany you on a walk to school or to your best friend's house. Draw a map below of your route.

GA1342

Follow the Route; Don't Pollute!

Enter the maze and draw a line to get to fresh air and a clean planet. Good luck on your journey!

Enter here.

GA1342

Days Gone By

The first gas station opened in Pittsburgh on December 1, 1913. Can you also find out when the first car was made? Write a report on your findings and also share your ideas about what life was like before cars.

Earthly Question: What is unleaded gasoline? _____

104

GA1342

Temps Up! Temps Up!

Air pollution turns clear, odorless air into dirty, smelly air that harms plants, burns lungs and eyes and hurts property. Did you know air pollution also affects the weather? Gases and particles in the air can cause changes in the average temperature. Particles in the air block the sun's rays so that temperatures may drop. Some gases like carbon dioxide permit sunlight to reach the earth but then trap the heat. This is called the *greenhouse effect*. How does the greenhouse effect change the average temperature?

_____

_____

_____

_____

Earthly Activity: Keep a weather chart for the next two weeks. Watch the weather report on local television each day. In one column put last year's high temperature for the date; in the other column this year's high temperature. Then add the numbers and divide by 14 to find the average high temperatures for the two-week period.

Day	High Temperature Last Year	High Temperature This Year
1		
2		
3		
4		
5		
6		
7		
8		
9		
10		
11		
12		
13		
14		
Total		

Divide by 14.

Average High Temperatures: Last Year _____ **This Year** _____

GA1342

Air Pollution

Most of the gases and particles humans put into the air come from combustion or burning. Where do we find furnaces? Factories have furnaces. Draw pictures of places and things where you live that burn fuel, chemicals or waste products.

GA1342

Earthly Reminders

Earthly Activity: Why do advertisers use pictures, slogans and jingles to describe their products? How do jingles help you remember the product?

Can you think of any slogans or jingles? Here are examples.

Good to the last drop.
Buckle up for safety.
An apple a day keeps the doctor away.
Don't leave home without it.

Everyone needs some help to remember to do what is right for planet Earth. Create three slogans that will help your schoolmates remember not to pollute. Plan to perform your jingle or slogan with a two to three-minute commercial or skit for your fellow students. Select your favorite to use as the basis for a billboard.

GA1342

Jump in on Junk Mail

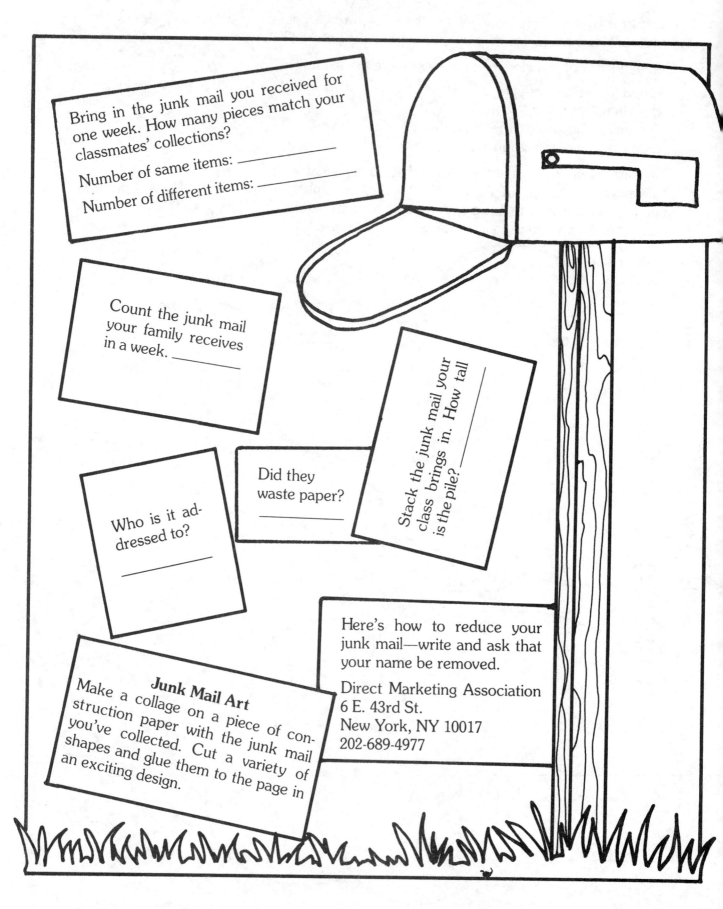

Bring in the junk mail you received for one week. How many pieces match your classmates' collections?

Number of same items: _____

Number of different items: _____

Count the junk mail your family receives in a week. _____

Stack the junk mail your class brings in. How tall is the pile? _____

Who is it addressed to?

_____

Did they waste paper?

_____

Here's how to reduce your junk mail—write and ask that your name be removed.

Direct Marketing Association
6 E. 43rd St.
New York, NY 10017
202-689-4977

Junk Mail Art
Make a collage on a piece of construction paper with the junk mail you've collected. Cut a variety of shapes and glue them to the page in an exciting design.

108

GA1342

Litter or Not? That Is the Question.

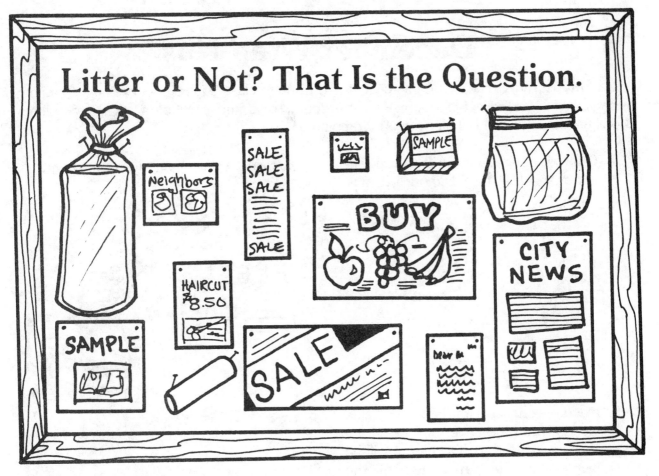

Ask students to bring in examples of junk mail their families receive in the mail. Cover the bulletin board with the collection. Talk about types of categories that could describe the pieces. Have the class generate a list of categories which might include coupons, advertisements, catalogs, requests from charities, etc. To whom is the mail addressed? Is it addressed to "occupant" or by name? Talk about the types of pieces brought in. Does everyone agree on what is junk mail? Is one person's junk mail, another person's information?

How would you classify the following examples? Are they junk mail?

A letter from a friend _____

An ad for groceries _____

A sample box of cereal _____

A bill _____

An announcement of the symphony schedule _____

A newspaper _____

The neighborhood newsletter _____

Coupons from stores in the neighborhood _____

A flyer from someone willing to mow lawns _____

GA1342

December Wrap-Ups

Earthly Activity: Have students collect and bring to class paper grocery bags, shopping bags, etc. Also collect old sponges, Styrofoam trays and cardboard scraps. Students will use these to make their own gift wrapping paper.

1. Cut the sponges and cardboard pieces into shapes like stars, diamonds, hearts, etc.

2. Paint the shapes with tempera paint.

3. Place the shapes with the painted side facedown on the paper and press the shape and lift it up. The design will be printed on the paper. Repeat the designs in a pattern.

110

GA1342

How Clean Are Our Oceans?

There is a lot of trash in the oceans. To know how much you must be able to read some **big** numbers.

10—ten
100—one hundred
1000—one thousand
10,000—ten thousand
100,000—one hundred thousand
1,000,000—one million
10,000,000—ten million
100,000,000—one hundred million
1,000,000,000—one billion
10,000,000,000—ten billion
100,000,000,000—one hundred billion
1,000,000,000,000—one trillion

Now you can read how much trash is put into the oceans each year. Read these numbers.

14,000,000,000 pounds of sewage
100,000,000 tons of plastic
165,710 tons of ship garbage
1 to 10,000,000 tons of oil

Are there more pounds of ships' garbage or more pounds of sewage in the ocean?

1 ton = 2000 pounds
1 ton of garbage = 2000 pounds of garbage

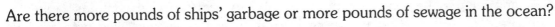

Translate the tons into pounds

165 tons = _____ pounds

20 tons = _____ pounds

5 tons = _____ pounds

166,000 pounds = _____ tons

20,000 pounds = _____ tons

86,000 pounds = _____ tons

Earth Alert: How many pounds of garbage go into the oceans each year? _____

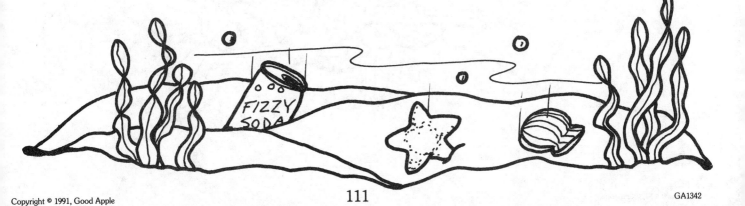

111

GA1342

To Sea or Not to Sea

Can you imagine going to the beach and not being able to swim? That is what has happened to many children along the eastern seaboard. They have found bags filled with medical debris—hypodermics, used waste, medications, etc.—floating to shore. Industrial factories have also poured their waste into the rivers for years.

Write a letter to your state congressman or senator, the president or chairman of the board of an industry about your environmental concerns.

112

GA1342

Earth Alert: To be taken seriously you must look serious. Congressmen and executives are busy people. Use the correct form for a business letter. Write legibly and get to the point!

Date _____

Address of person _____
to whom you _____
are sending _____
the letter _____

Dear _____ :

_____
_____
_____
_____
_____
_____
_____

Salutation

Name

Address

_____
_____

113

GA1342

Music to Our Earth Ears

On December 16th, Ludwig van Beethoven was born in the year of 1770. His music filled the air with lovely melodious sounds. Who are your favorite composers? What is music to your ears now may be harmful to your ears over time. A person can barely hear sounds of zero decibels. Sounds about 130 decibels can be painful to the ears. Some rock musicians have lost their hearing by being exposed to very loud music over the years.

What Is Music to Your Ears?	What Is Noise to Your Ears?
1.	1.
2.	2.
3.	3.
4.	4.
5.	5.
6.	6.

GA1342

Noisy or Not?

Earth Alert: Noise pollution is a problem in urban areas. Loud noises are annoying and may also harm your ears. Noises are measured in units called *decibels*. Add your list of music and noises to the chart below.

"Noise"

jet plane (nearby), very loud rock music

_____

_____

_____

jackhammer

_____

_____

_____

car horn

_____

_____

_____

vacuum

_____

_____

_____

whispering

_____

_____

_____

160

100

60

0

ROAR!

HONK!

PSST

GA1342

December Wraps It Up!

Students will enjoy this bulletin board as you encourage them to write a story about their previous year on earth. How did they help the earth; how did they contribute their efforts to save its treasures? Display the stories on the board. Duplicate a present pattern for each child from the pattern below and add his name. Pass the presents around the room and let fellow students write their holiday wishes or tips for the earth.

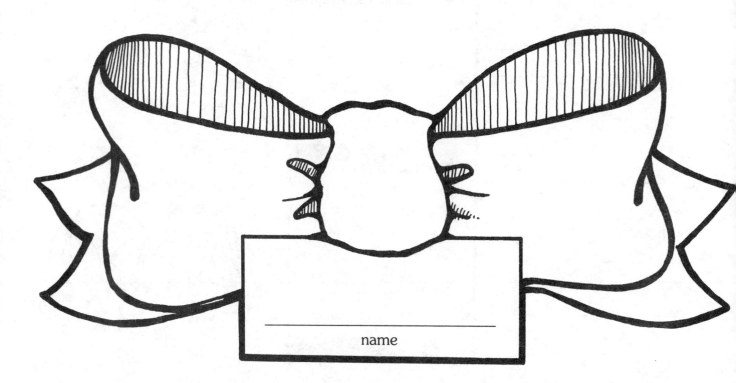

name

Miracles Old and New

Two special holidays occur during December—Christmas and Hanukkah. Christmas celebrates the miracle of the birth of Jesus.

Hanukkah, the Festival of Lights, is a Jewish holiday which begins on the eve of the 25th day of the Hebrew month of Kislev. The holiday celebrates the miracle that a small band of men were able to defend themselves against a large army of soldiers and that a small vial of oil was able to stay lit in the Everlasting Light of the Great Temple until more sacred oil could be gotten.

Planet Earth needs a few miracles to survive. Draw pictures of the miracles you wish for planet Earth. At the bottom of the picture write your miracle wish.

117

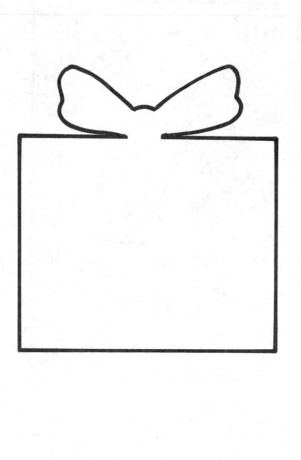

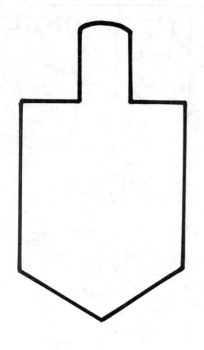

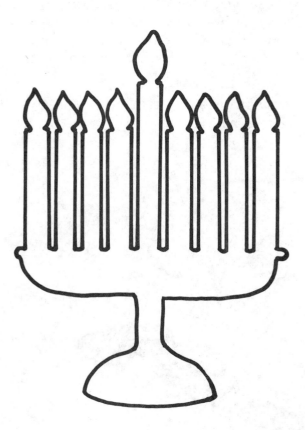

GA1342

"Tree"mendous Greetings in December!

Here's the ideal bulletin board for recycling old greeting cards and for saving trees. Make ornaments by cutting up greeting cards and making them into colorful ornaments. Add them to the Christmas tree during the month of December.

Tip: Make a 3″ (7.6 cm) slit from top to (near) bottom of one cutout and one from bottom to top in the second cutout. Slide the two pieces together to make three-dimensional ornaments for the tree.

119

GA1342

Season's Greetings

Write a special message to each of these earth's treasures. Your seasonal greeting could be a wish, your thoughts or idea to help it.

Season's Greetings to the Earth

Season's Greetings to a Tree

Season's Greetings to Endangered Species

Season's Greetings to the Ocean

Season's Greetings to Air

GA1342

The Pollution Patrol

Earth to Student: Use this story starter to get you started, and write a story about your experience while working on the pollution patrol.

I was so surprised when I discovered _____

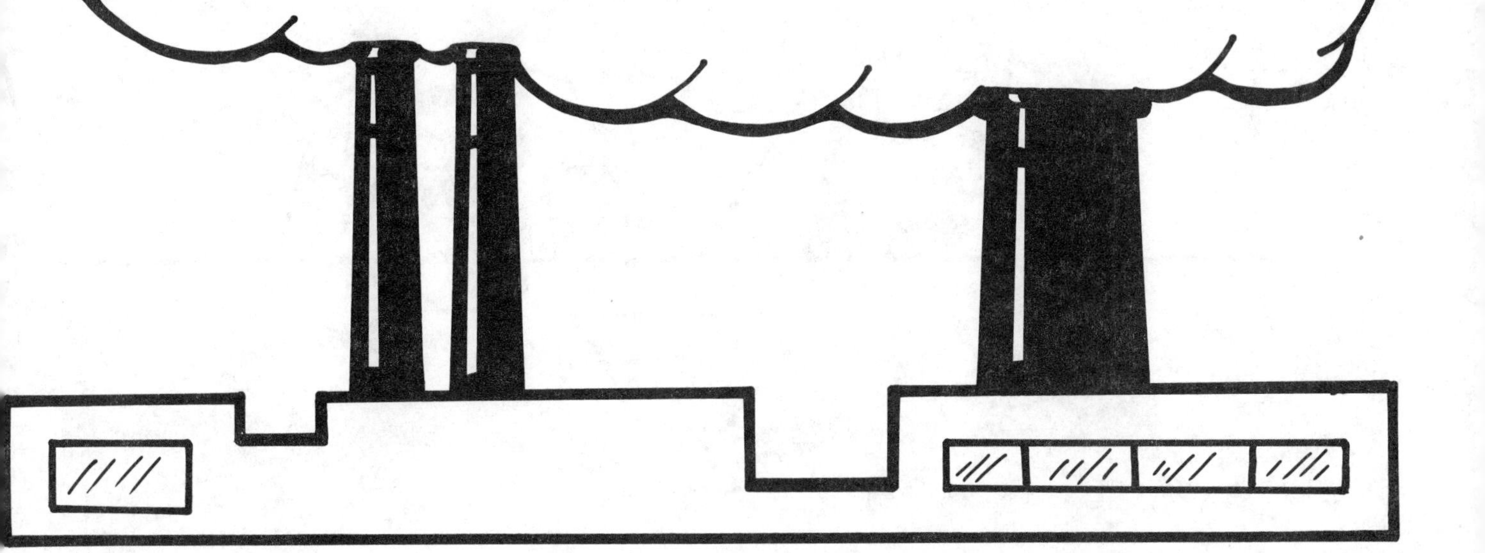

_____

_____

_____

_____

_____

_____

_____

_____

_____

_____

_____

_____

_____

_____

Wishing for a Happy New Year

There are sad stories and happy stories. Choose a partner. Together turn one of these stories around to give it a happy ending in the new year.

It was a very sad day. When the children went to the beach, the sand was covered with plastic bags, used hypodermic needles and other medical supplies that had washed up onto the shore.

"I am RX597 from the planet Xenon. I want to learn about your planet. What are all these little pieces of paper on the street? Why are they there?"

"When I was a little boy, many years ago, there were many kinds of animals we don't have now. And lots of people kept pets, but because no one took care of planet Earth, there are no more dogs now . . ."

"The smog has gotten so bad in my city that we all wear masks when we go out. Still our clothes get sooty. We asked the city council . . ."

122

GA1342

Litter Line Up

Encourage students to collect trash that they find around the school and at home. Make sure there are no sharp edges or rusty cans. Concentrate on paper and plastic. Have students bring in the trash and pin it to the bulletin board. When the board is covered, award each student with the badge of honor below.

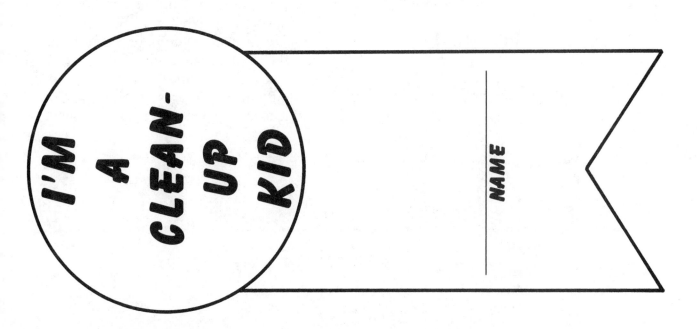

December De"lights" Us!

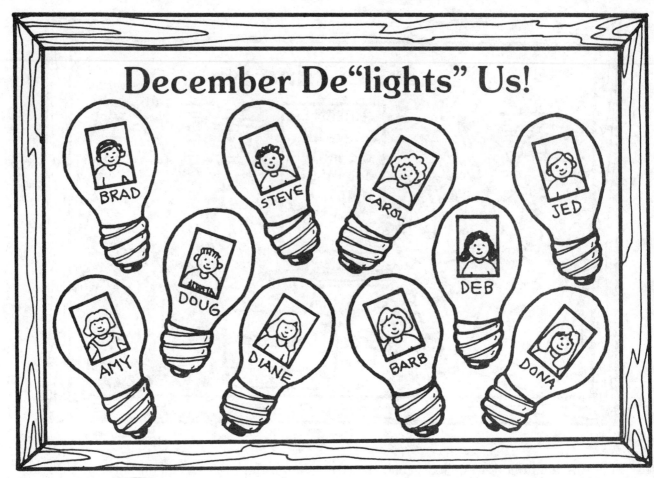

Add student's picture here.

_____
Student's name

Use this bulletin board to introduce your students to enlightening ideas about ways to help clean up the environment. Shed some light on this subject and encourage students to brighten up the earth by not littering and keeping it clean. Students could have a school grounds cleanup and schedule a special time for collecting trash and picking up litter. Add students' photographs or pictures of them cleaning up the school grounds to their light bulbs.

GA134

This Room Has Class!

Earth to Student: You can set a good example by keeping your desk and classroom neat. Each time you do something that contributes to a clean room environment, color in a star.

Star Student

125

GA1342

Earthly Project: Students, here is your chance to create an environmentally aware classroom mascot. Give him a name, a costume and think about how he should look since he's helping to save the earth!

126

Helping the Earth Is My Bag

Earth to Student: You can help keep the earth clean in lots of ways. This is your bag! Fill the bag with illustrations or write ideas of all the things you have learned this fall to help keep the earth looking beautiful.

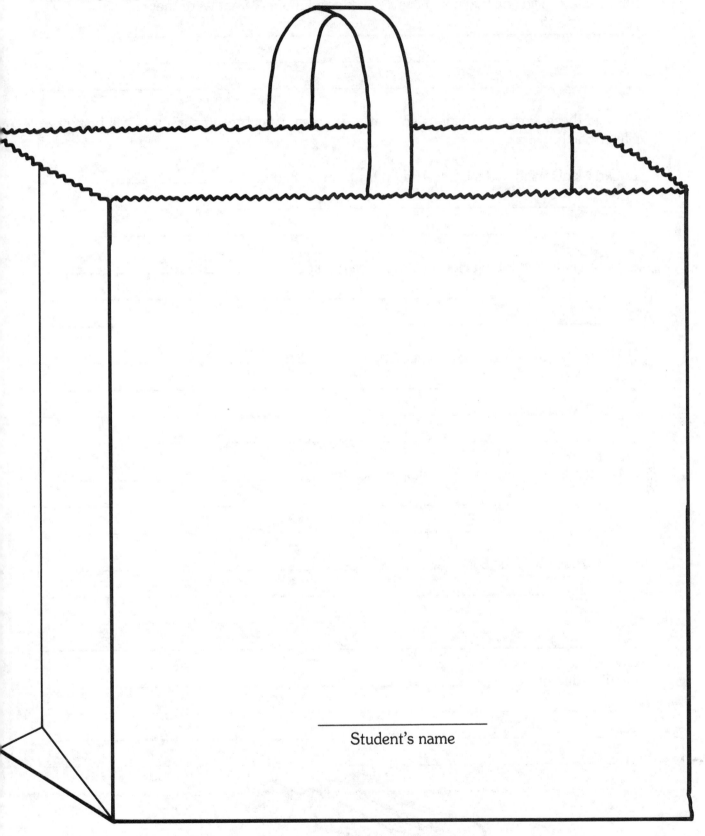

Student's name

127

It's a New Year!

Sometimes people make New Year's resolutions about how they will act differently in the new year. Did you make any New Year's resolutions? What were they?

_____

_____

_____

Change these stories and songs so that in the new year these characters will help save planet Earth.

1. Old MacDonald had a farm. And on his farm he had _____

_____

_____

2. When little Red Riding Hood entered the forest _____

_____

_____

3. When the three bears got home _____

_____

_____

_____

4. Cinderella outgrew her glass slippers so she _____

_____

_____

5. Row, row, row your boat _____

_____

_____

_____

6. Rub-a-dub-dub _____

_____

_____

_____

128

GA1342

What on Earth You Can Do in

January

Earth Words for January

Electricity: Power that comes from the movement of tiny particles called electrons

Energy: A source that enables work to be done

Energy Supply: The total amount of energy available for use

Insulation: Material used to prevent energy loss

Fossil Fuels: Fuels developed from remnants of prehistoric plants and animals. Fossil fuels include coal, oil and natural gas.

Efficiency: Using the lowest amount of energy possible to get the work done

Nuclear Energy: Energy that comes from the splitting of certain atoms

Solar Energy: Energy provided through the power of the sun

Geothermal Power: Power generated when water comes into contact with heated rocks within the earth and causes steam to be formed

Conservation: The actions taken to preserve earth's natural resources

Crude Oil: Oil pumped directly from the ground

Global Warming: The tendency of the earth's average temperature to rise because of air pollution

GA1342

Match Them Up

Use the clues to unscramble the words and match the word to its definition.

Power that comes from the movement of electrons

A source to get work done

Material that protects for energy loss

Energy provided by the sun's power

The tendency of the earth's average temperature to rise

Fuels developed millions of years ago from the remains of animals and plants

Petroleum

tionnisUlA _____

EyenGr _____

loaBgl Mawring _____

Sloar eEgryn _____

loi _____

sloifs Sluef _____

cityerleCti _____

131

Do a Power Survey

Look around your classroom. How many things in your classroom require electricity to run? Fill in the classroom with the objects you find.

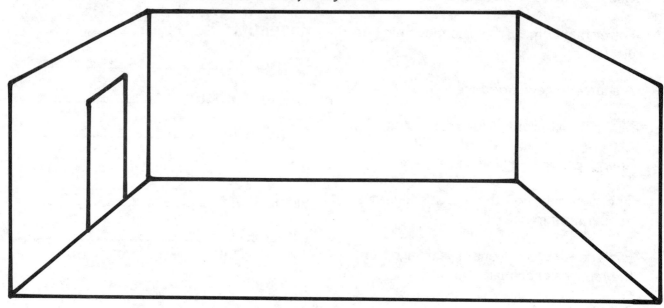

Earth to Homework: Do a power survey of your home. Fill in the rooms of the house below with all the items you find that need electricity.

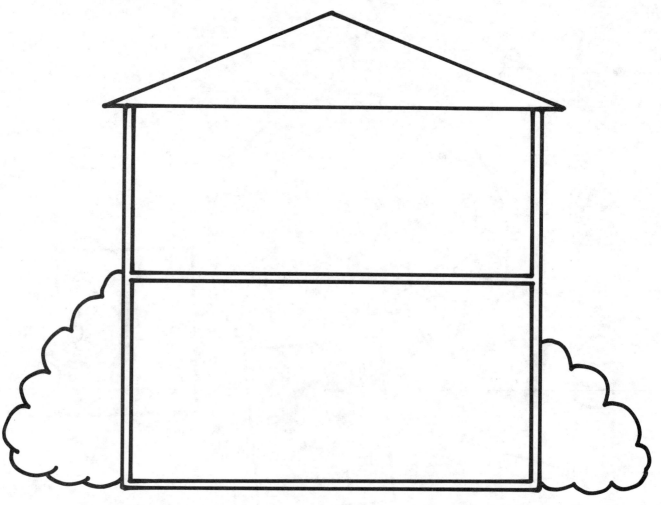

GA1342

How Much Electricity Do You Use?

Earth to Homework: Where does your electricity come from?

_____

What is the name of your power company?

_____

Ask your parents to show you how to read the electric meter. Do the dials on the meter look like the ones below?

The dials show kilowatt hours used. A kilowatt hour is the amount of energy present in one kilowatt of electricity for one hour.

The dials above read 26930.

What do the dials on your family's meter read? _____

One week from today read the meter again? _____

Subtract the first amount from the second to determine how many kilowatts of electricity your family used in one week.

To find out how much a kilowatt costs, look at the electric bill. Multiply the amount the company charges per kilowatt by the number of kilowatts used to determine how much the electricity your family used in one week costs.

GA1342

Lights, Camera, Action

Earth to Student: Get into action and help save energy. When the lights are on, you are using electricity. Put the spotlight on saving it and keep a record of every time you conserve electricity in your home. Color a light bulb to show your progress and list what you did.

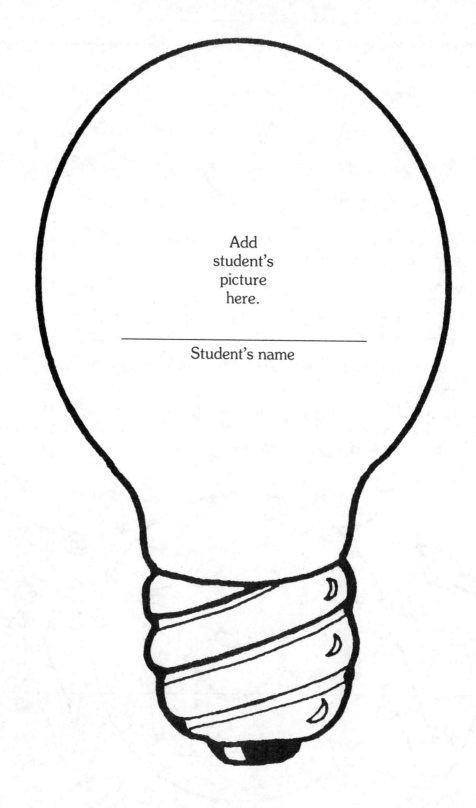

Add
student's
picture
here.

_____

Student's name

GA1342

Light Up!

Earth to Homework: Fluorescent bulbs last longer and use less energy than conventional incandescent light bulbs. Each fluorescent bulb lasts ten times longer than regular bulbs. Count the number of incandescent light bulbs in your home?

How many are there? _____

If you change each bulb, it will cost a lot of money. How much more does a fluorescent bulb cost than an incandescent one? _____

If you save $40 over the lifetime of each bulb (because you won't have to change it as often), how much money will your family save?

_____ × ____40____ = $
Number of
  bulbs

GA1342

Count the Miles

One way to save energy is to use fuel-efficient cars. How much gasoline does your family's car use each week? How many miles can your car go on one tank of gas? To be really fuel efficient, some people think a car should be able to go 35 miles on one gallon of gas. Figure out how many miles to the gallon your car can go.

Look at this odometer.

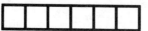

It reads thirty-seven thousand two hundred and thirty-three and 3 tenths miles. The last number on the right counts the tenths of a mile the car goes.

Ask your parent to take you to the filling station when he/she fills the car with gasoline the next time. Record what the odometer says in the odometer below.

When the car needs gas again, fill in the odometer.

How many gallons of gasoline did you have to buy to refill the tank? _____

Determine the number of miles per gallon your car will drive by dividing the number of gallons of gas you used into the number of miles that were driven between fill-ups.

Is your car fuel efficient? _____

GA1342

Think Tank

Miles Traveled	How Many Miles Does the Car Get for a Gallon of Gas?	How Many Gallons of Gas Will You Need?
10	17	
80	18	
600	20	
126	14	
190	20	
64	16	
50	18	
190	19	
200	20	

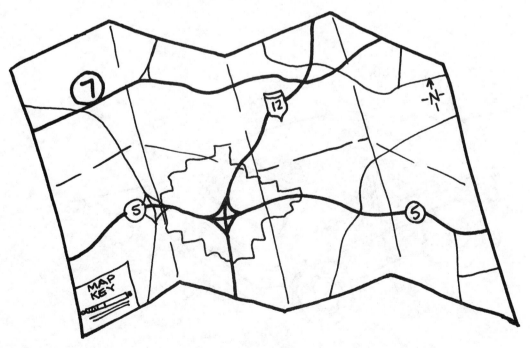

GA1342

It's a Gas!

Earth to Student: Ask your parent to help you find how many miles (kilometers) he/she drives each day. Add up the amounts and divide by the number of days to find the average. Compare your answers with your classmates'.

Miles (Kilometers) Driven

Monday _____

Tuesday _____

Wednesday _____

Thursday _____

Friday _____

Total = _____

Average = _____

GA1342

Go, Go Graph

How many miles does your family car travel each day?

Earth to Student: List your results on the graph.

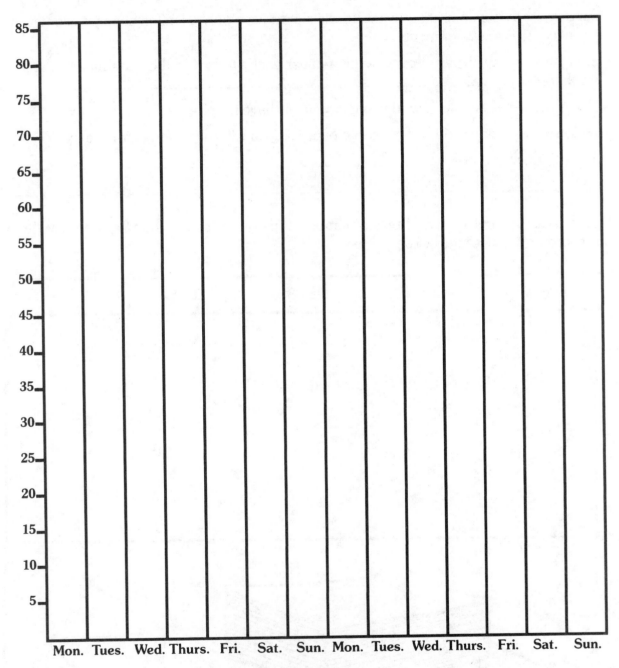

GA1342

How Little Is There?

The **energy supply** is the total amount of energy available for people to use. Over 90 percent of the energy we use comes from **fossil fuels** like coal, oil and natural gas. These fuels are developed from the fossilized remains of prehistoric animals and plants. The earth has only a limited supply of fossil fuels. Someday the supply will be gone. What do you think that will be like?

Earthly Activity: To find out what it feels like to have only a limited supply of something you need, try this experiment.

Count how many pieces of clean writing paper each student in the class has. How many are there? _____

This is the whole supply of writing paper you will have for one week.

What are some ways you can conserve paper so you will have enough for the week? ____

What else can you do? _____

_____

Keep a diary about the week of the number of pieces of paper you use each day. Keep a record of your feelings below.

Day 1	Day 2	Day 3	Day 4	Day 5

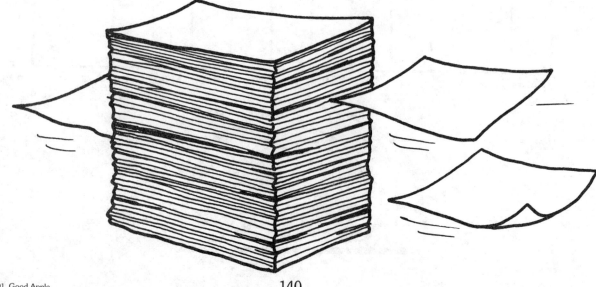

GA1342

Total These Energy Savers!

The problems in parentheses are for older students.

My family walked to the store. My mother, father and two sisters went with me. How many of us went for the walk? (If the grocery store is 2.4 miles [3.86 km] away and if we walk there 4 times this week, how many miles [kilometers] will everyone walk?)	We lowered our thermostat setting to 76° F (24.4° C). It was at 80° F (26.4° C). How many degrees did we lower it? (If we used 1 percent less energy each month, how much less energy will we use for the year?)
My friend Bob, two adults and our teacher took a shortcut. How many people saved energy? (Potential energy is stored energy. Kinetic energy is energy of motion. What kind of energy do we use when we walk?)	Justin is reading a book on saving the earth. The book has 105 pages. He is on page 62. How many pages does he have left to read? (If there is an average of 200 words on each page, how many words does he have left to read?)
Last weekend my mother opened up the refrigerator 5 times, and I opened it up 8 times. How many times did we open it? (If each time we opened the door it was left open at least ½ minute, how long was it left open?)	Last week we walked to the school playground 10 times, and we walked to school 8 times. How many times did we walk in all? (The school playground is 475 yards [432.25 m] across. It is 1 yard [.91 m] to school. How far did we all walk?)

GA1342

A"mazing" Energy

Conserve on energy and find the shortest route as you enter this maze.

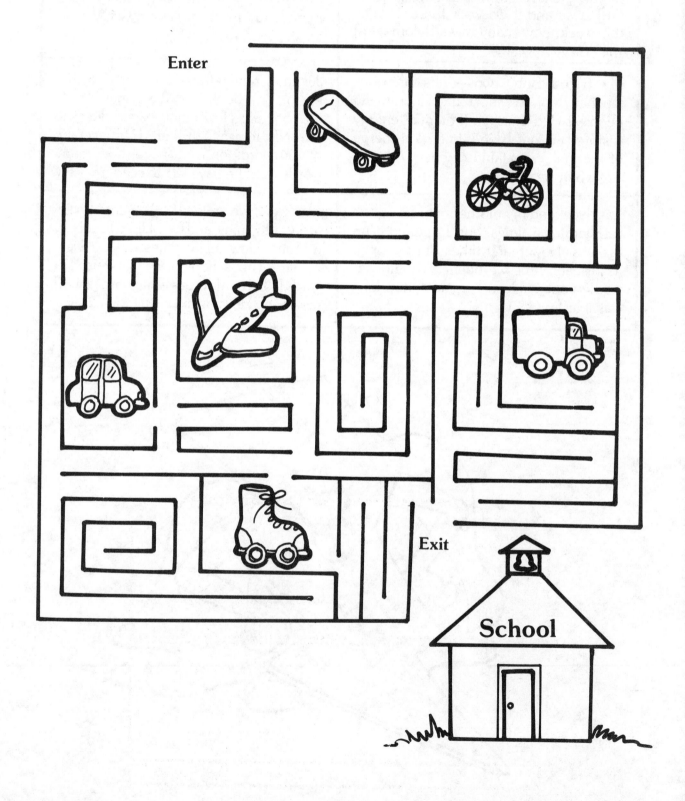

GA1342

Heat Busters

Earth to Student: Listen to the heat run in your house. When the furnace is running, energy is being used. Time the furnace as it runs during a one-hour period.

Did it stay on most of the hour?

What would happen if you turned up the thermostat? Would the furnace run more or less if you turned down the thermostat?

Earth to Homework: At a family meeting, identify realistic ways your family can use less energy at home. Bring the list to school. Compile the lists and take home the new ideas.

My family agrees to save energy by:

1. _____
2. _____
3. _____
4. _____
5. _____
6. _____
7. _____
8. _____
9. _____
10. _____

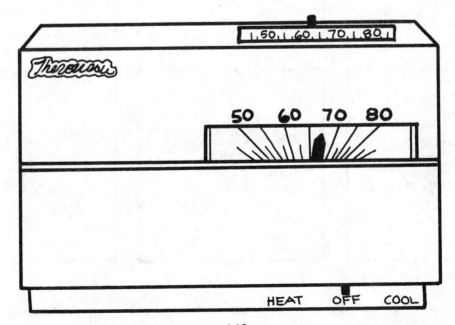

GA1342

Refrigerator Calculator

Earth to Student: Every time you open the refrigerator, you lose energy. Calculate the answers to these questions and compare your results with your classmates'.

? ? ? ? ? ?

ON	Total times I opened it	Time of day my family opened the refrigerator the most
OFF	Why did I open it?	Who leaves the refrigerator open while putting items on the counter?
	Time of day I opened the refrigerator	Total times they opened it

144

Refrigerator Navigator

Earth to Student: How can you open the refrigerator less times? Brainstorm your ideas with your family and list your solutions here.

1. _____
_____
_____

2. _____
_____
_____

3. _____
_____
_____

4. _____
_____
_____

5. _____
_____
_____

6. _____
_____
_____

7. _____
_____
_____

8. _____
_____
_____

GA1342

Closed and Shut Case

Earth to Student: Draw a sign to be posted on your refrigerator to help remind your family to open the refrigerator less often.

GA1342

Figuring Percentages

Petroleum furnishes almost half of the energy used in the world. What does your family use petroleum for?

_____

_____

Coal provides about 30 percent of the energy used in the world. What does your family use coal for?

_____

_____

Natural gas supplies about 20 percent of the energy used in the world. What does your family use natural gas for?

_____

_____

If you consider all of your family's energy needs equal 100 percent, what percentages of the other fossil fuels does your family use? Remember the percentages can only add up to 100 percent if these are the only fuels you use.

Petroleum

Coal

Natural Gas

What other energy sources does your family depend on? Circle them below.

Electricity

Nuclear Power

Solar Power

Wind Power

Geothermal Energy

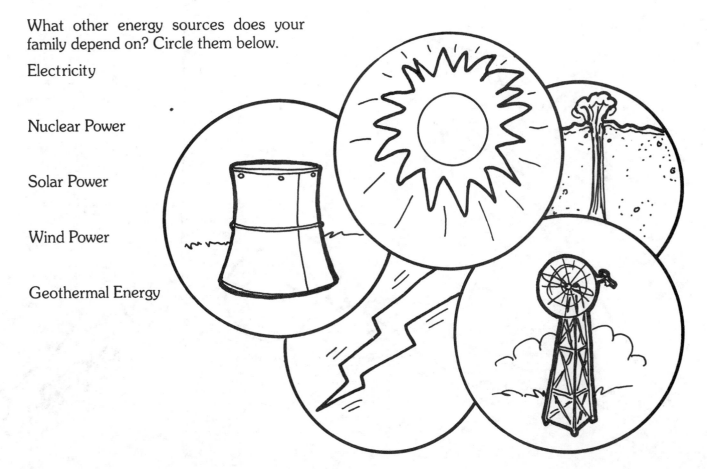

GA1342

A Sad Day

March 24, 1989, was a very sad day for Alaska. On that day a ship ran into a reef and spilled millions of gallons of crude oil into Prince William Sound.

Many, many animals were killed. The oil spill ruined the beaches and destroyed the homes of many animals. Oil companies are always looking for more oil to pump. Now oil companies want to find more oil in Alaska. To get companies to pump less oil, we must use less oil. List the ways we can use less oil.

1. _____

_____

2. _____

_____

3. _____

_____

4. _____

_____

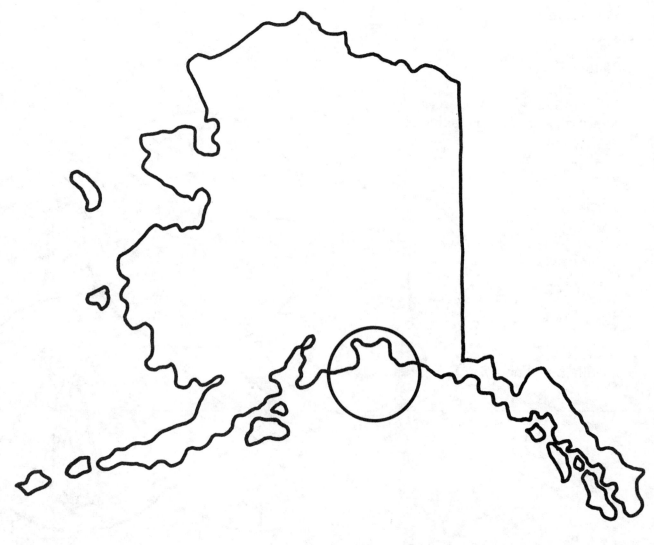

Batteries Up!

A battery is a container that makes electricity because of the way the chemicals inside it react to each other. What are some items that use batteries?

Earth to Homework: List all the items in your house that use batteries.

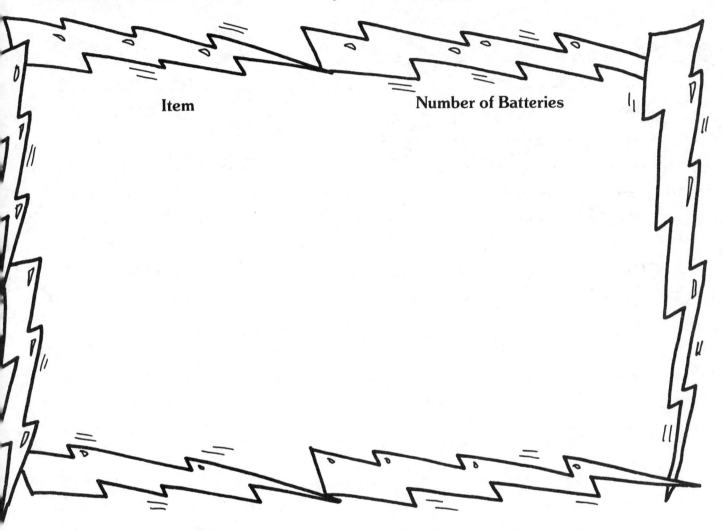

Item	Number of Batteries

Batteries only work as long as the chemicals inside them react. Batteries often are filled with toxic chemicals that can pollute if they are not disposed of properly.

What are two ways to make batteries last longer?

1. _____

_____

2. _____

_____

Batteries Up!

A battery is a container that makes electricity because of the way the chemicals inside it react to each other. What are some items that use batteries?

Earth to Homework: List all the items in your house that use batteries.

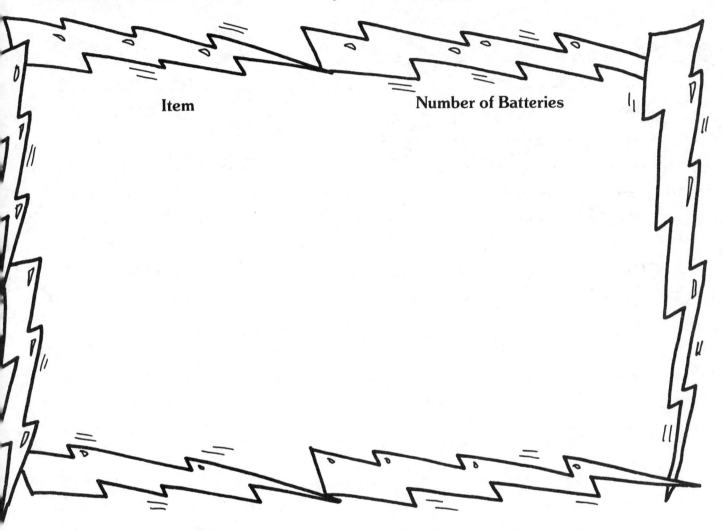

Item   Number of Batteries

Batteries only work as long as the chemicals inside them react. Batteries often are filled with toxic chemicals that can pollute if they are not disposed of properly.

What are two ways to make batteries last longer?

1. _____

_____

2. _____

_____

GA1342

Renew It!

Some energy sources are *renewable*. Solar energy and wind power are both plentiful and don't harm the environment.

Re- is a prefix. It means "again."

Add *re-* to each word below and use it in a sentence.

new _____   _____

_____

use _____   _____

_____

play _____   _____

_____

do _____   _____

_____

call _____   _____

_____

cook _____   _____

_____

visit _____   _____

_____

BOOK OF PREFIXES

GA1342

Nature's Cover-Ups

Earth to Student: When it is cold outside you wear a coat to stay warm, but how do the trees, animals and things in nature stay warm? List your ideas here. Can you draw pictures to illustrate your ideas?

Clues: What do bark, snow and fur protect? What does *hibernate* mean?

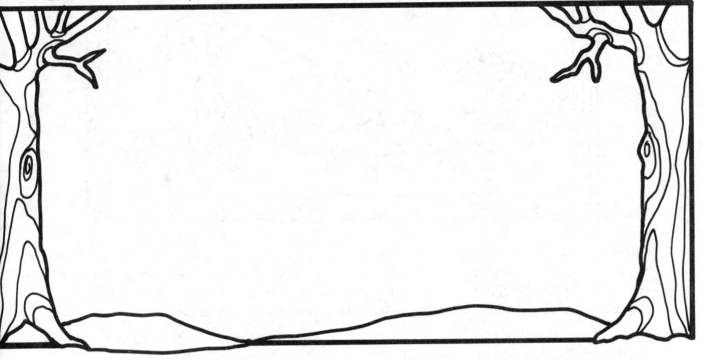

Earthly Idea: Can you take a tip from nature? When it is cold outside, what can you do so you can still save energy indoors?

Solar energy comes from the "sun"sational sun. Here's an example of a bulletin board to teach your students this fact. *Solar energy* is energy produced by the sun. The sun can start a fire; it can make someone feel warm. The sun's rays can be collected in large flat panels called solar collectors and transformed into electricity.

Give each student a copy of the sun pattern below. Ask the students to invent a device that could use the sun's energy to power it.

GA1342

New Year's Resolutions

Earth to Student: Make family resolutions on how you can help save the earth's treasures.

The _____ Family's New Year's Resolutions

1. _____

_____

_____

_____

2. _____

_____

_____

_____

3. _____

_____

_____

_____

GA1342

Conservation Delegation

Join the conservation delegation and every time you conserve energy, recycle or help save the earth's treasures, cast a vote for yourself and color in a star. Write what you did below the star.

154

Electrifying Experiment

Earth Alert: For one evening try to use nothing that needs electricity. It will be hard. What can't you use? What did you do instead?

GA1342

I'm a Smart Cookie

I'm a smart cookie. Here is how I'm helping the earth! List your ideas on the cookies below.

Earthly Idea: Ask your friend for a favorite cookie recipe. Swap recipes; then help Mom make them!

GA1342

Lights Out

Now you are ready to finish the story and write what it'd be like without electricity.

Once upon a time there was no electricity. _____

_____

_____

_____

_____

_____

_____

_____

_____

_____

_____

_____

_____

_____

_____

_____

_____

_____

_____

GA1342

Energizing Books

This bulletin board will introduce students to some exciting books. Ask each child to select an adventure book or action book. Have each student draw a picture, write a paragraph and plan a one-minute presentation about the most exciting thing that happened in the book. Display the book reports on the bulletin board.

Name of book: _____

Author: _____

The most exciting thing that happened in this book was _____

_____

_____

_____

_____

_____

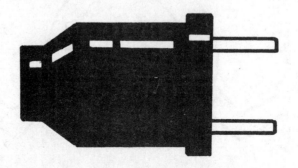

GA1342

Earth Award

Earth to Student: Color this award and fill out the bottom part with ways you are helping.

Ask Me How I Am Helping the Earth

Cut out this award and wear it!

Every day can be Earth Day!

GA1342

Be a Super Saver

Earth to Student: Design a badge your classmates and you can earn by being an energy saver.

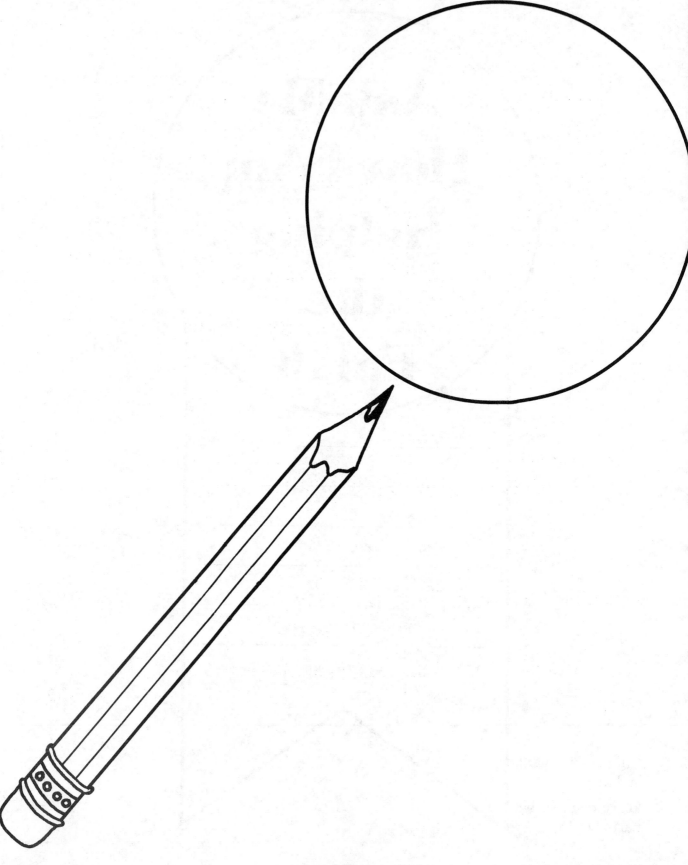

GA1342

What on Earth You Can Do in

February

Earth Words for February

Reservoir: A place where water is collected and stored

Water Main: The largest pipe carrying water to a community

Evaporate: To heat a substance like water so that it is changed into a gas or vapor

Filter: A device through which liquid is passed to remove any impurities

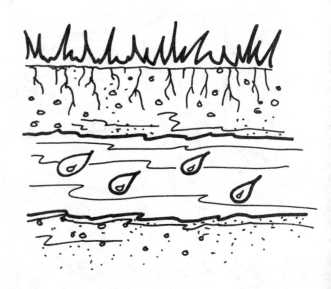

Pollutants: Any harmful substance which harms a natural resource like water or air

Source: A place from which something comes

Water Meter: A device that measures how much water is being used

Chlorine: A chemical that is added to water to clean it

Groundwater: Water that is found in natural reservoirs under the earth

Oil Slick: A film of oil that forms on a body of water after oil is dumped into the water

Water Cycle: The continuous process by which water evaporates, forms clouds, rains and then returns to streams and bodies of water before starting the cycle again

GA1342

Superb Sentences

When every word in a phrase or sentence begins with the same letter, it is called *alliteration*. Use each word below in a sentence with as many words as possible beginning with the same letter as each word.

Example:

water: **W**hen **we** **w**aste **w**ater **we** **w**onder **w**hat **w**ent **w**rong.

save: _____

_____

rain: _____

_____

pollutant: _____

_____

energy: _____

_____

filter: _____

_____

conservation: _____

_____

leak: _____

_____

faucet: _____

_____

GA1342

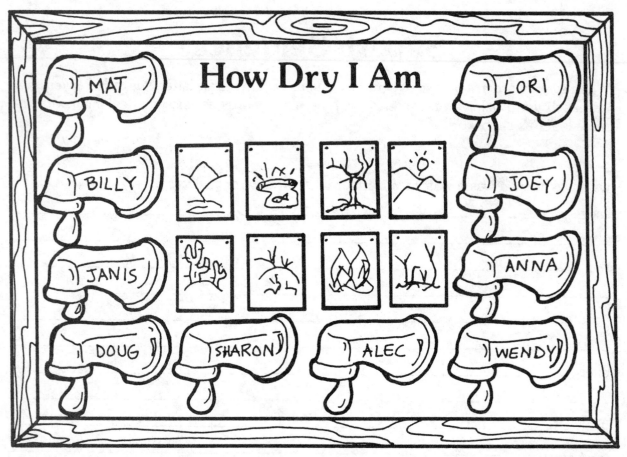

How Dry I Am

MAT
BILLY
JANIS
DOUG
SHARON
ALEC
WENDY
ANNA
JOEY
LORI

Use this bulletin board to encourage students to use less water. Students can illustrate what the earth would look like if there were no water. Display the pictures on the bulletin board. Each time a student puts a water-saving idea into action, let him sign his name on his water faucet. Line the bulletin board border with a faucet for each student.

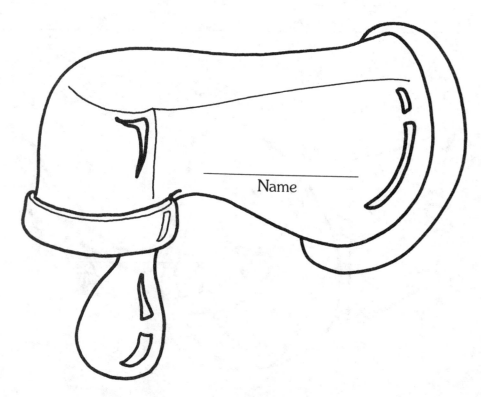

Name _____

164

GA1342

Watery Facts

Earth to Student: Hop from lily pad to lily pad. For each fact about our water consumption, write a solution to save water.

A washing machine can use 50 gallons (189 l) of water per load.

_____

A major use of water in neighborhoods goes to watering lawns.

_____

Every time you flush the toilet it uses 5-7 gallons (18.9-26.46 l) of water.

_____

An average bathtub holds 40 gallons (151.2 l) of water. A brief shower usually uses less water.

_____

A small leak can waste 20 gallons (75.6 l) of water a day.

_____

A lot of water is unused as it runs down the drain. It goes directly from faucet to drain as you brush your teeth, wash dishes or wash your face.

_____

When you water plants with a hose, some of the water is lost or cannot be absorbed.

_____

165

GA1342

Inspector H₂O

Be a water inspector and list all the objects and activities in your house that require water. Draw a picture of each in the water drops.

Add up the drops. How many drops did you find? _____

GA1342

The Conservative Detective

Put on your Sherlock Holmes hat and a super sleuth you can be.

- Where are the leaky faucets in your house? Write the names of the rooms on the faucets.

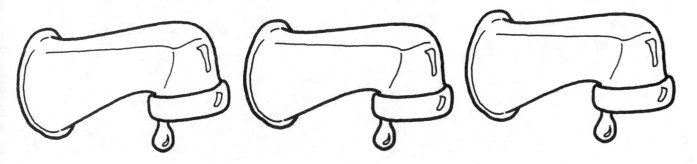

- Check the toilets for leaks. Put food coloring in the toilet tank. Wait fifteen minutes. If the water in the toilet bowl has become colored, you have a small leak. A leaky toilet can waste up to 100 gallons (378 l) of water a day! How many leaky toilets did you find?

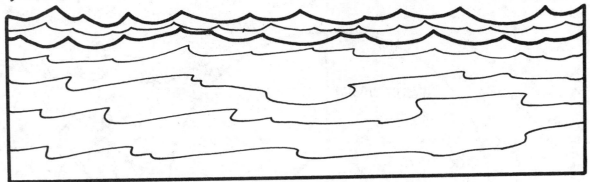

- One good deed deserves another. How many leaky toilets do you think there are in the school? Write a letter to the principal with class findings.

GA1342

The Water Cycle

The sun heats and evaporates the water in the ocean, lakes and streams. The water vapor rises and is absorbed by the clouds. When the clouds absorb so much water they cannot hold anymore, the clouds release the water in the form of rain. The rain falls to earth where some of it finally makes its way back to streams, lakes and other bodies of water.

Use the picture clues to help you fill in the waterwheel to explain the water cycle. The first step is done for you.

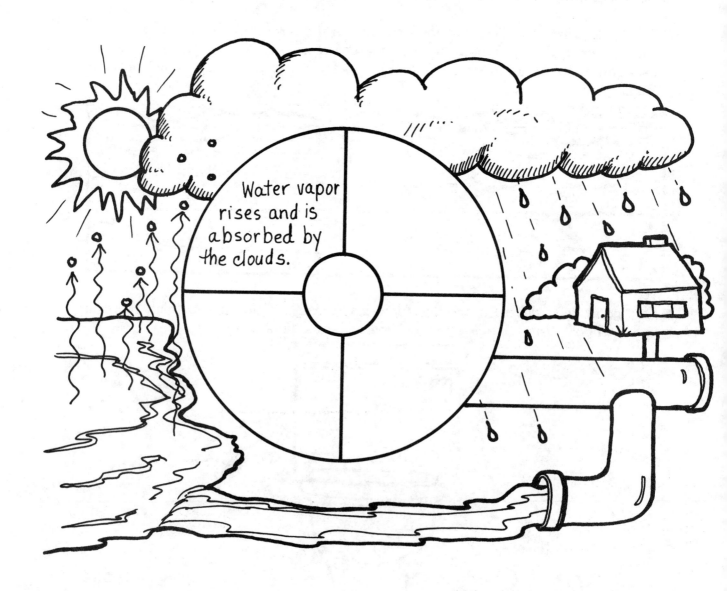

Water vapor rises and is absorbed by the clouds.

GA1342

Discovering Shower Power

Earth to Homework: A ten-minute shower can use 100 gallons (378 l) of water. Put a bucket under the shower head. How long does it take to fill up?

How many gallons of water does the bucket hold?

Week 1

Fill in the chart below with the length of time your shower lasts each day. Then *estimate* how much water you used during that shower.

Monday	Tuesday	Wednesday	Thursday	Friday

Total water used Week 1: _____

Week 2

Every time you shower, set a timer for a number of minutes one half to one third less than you showered before. Or choose the time of your shortest shower time last week. Shower for the same length of time every day.

Fill in the chart with the number of minutes you showered each day and the estimated amount of water used.

Monday	Tuesday	Wednesday	Thursday	Friday

Total water used Week 2: _____

How much water did you save? _____

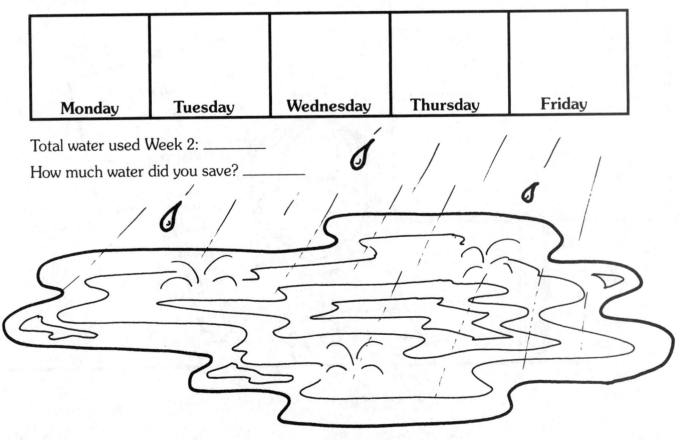

GA1342

Super Slogans

Help save water! Create slogans to encourage others to join in your effort.*

Shorter
Showers
Give
Water Power!

*Post your signs in appropriate places at home and school.

170

Water, Water Everywhere

Is water everywhere? Is it safe to drink the water from the pond in the park? What about in the stream down in the woods or in the neighborhood swimming pool? Why not?

_____

_____

What might happen if you drink water that is not clean?

_____

_____

Where does your water come from?

_____

_____

Most people in the United States get their water from a city water supply. What is the name on the water bill your familly gets? _____

Some systems take their water from underground streams or wells, others get it from nearby rivers or lakes and still others must pipe in water from faraway sources. Where does your city's water system get its water? _____

Draw a map of your city. Indicate the source of your city's water supply on the map. Is it a river, an underground source or is the water piped in?

The water from lakes and rivers is not pure enough to drink. It may have pollutants or bacteria in it. The water company takes the water and purifies it before piping it to your home. Chemicals are added to the water; then the water is left to sit so the impurities can collect. The water is filtered then treated again with chemicals. Now the water is placed in large reservoirs or tanks until it is ready to be piped to you.

GA1342

Find That Source

Look on a map of the United States. Which of the cities below have major rivers or lakes nearby? Draw in any large bodies of water that are near each city. What other large cities in the United States have a major body of water nearby?

GA1342

A Wet Tale

Cut out the pictures below and put them in the correct order to tell the story of how water gets from a river to your house.

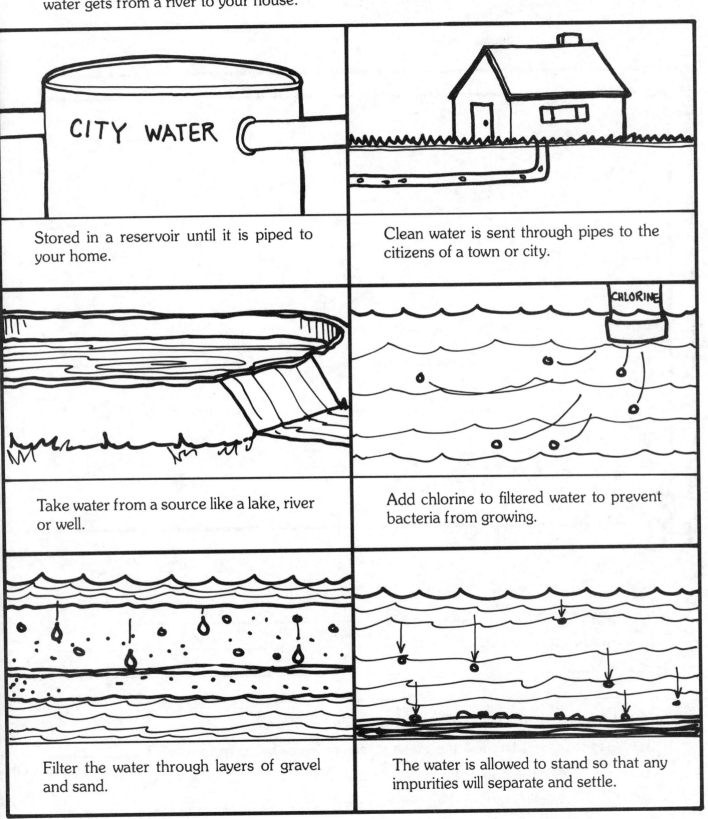

Stored in a reservoir until it is piped to your home.

Clean water is sent through pipes to the citizens of a town or city.

Take water from a source like a lake, river or well.

Add chlorine to filtered water to prevent bacteria from growing.

Filter the water through layers of gravel and sand.

The water is allowed to stand so that any impurities will separate and settle.

GA1342

Wondering About Water

Earth to Homework: Enlist the help of an adult to answer these questions. Compare your results with your classmates'.

Where is the water meter in your home? _____

Draw a picture of the water meter.

How does it work? _____

_____

_____

_____

Take a reading on the meter when you get up in the morning. _____

What is the reading on the water meter when you come home from school? _____

How much does water cost? _____

What is your family's water bill for one month? _____

GA1342

Earth Lovers Unite

Earth to Student: Think of ways you can help save the earth and its treasures. Create earth lovers' valentines. Fill in the examples on this page; color them in and cut them out.

Be a Super Sailor

Help Columbus sail the ocean blue and put an *X* on each item that would pollute the water.

176

GA1342

Join the Water Saver's Club

Circle the ways to conserve water.

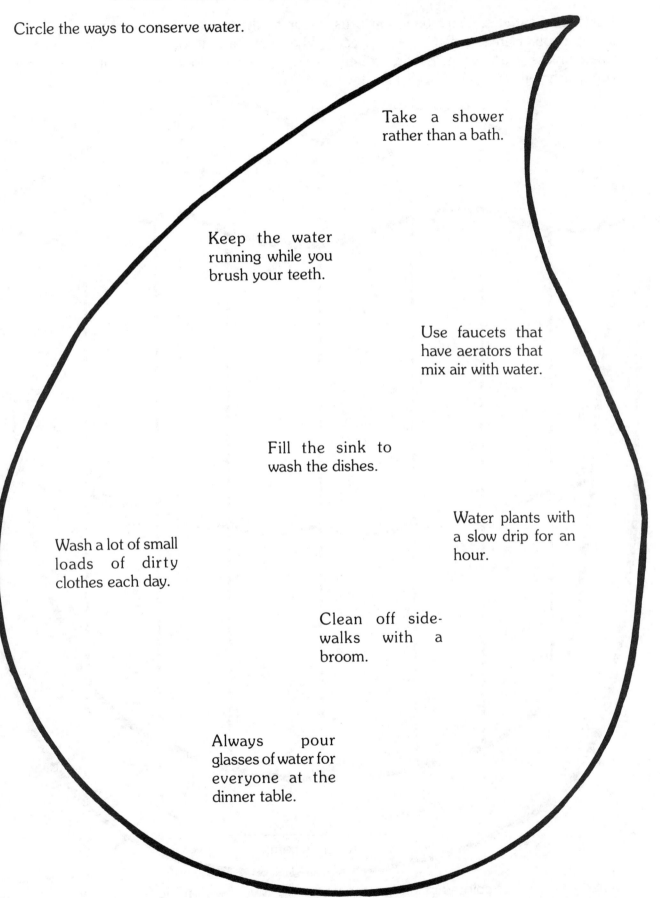

Take a shower rather than a bath.

Keep the water running while you brush your teeth.

Use faucets that have aerators that mix air with water.

Fill the sink to wash the dishes.

Water plants with a slow drip for an hour.

Wash a lot of small loads of dirty clothes each day.

Clean off side-walks with a broom.

Always pour glasses of water for everyone at the dinner table.

GA1342

Be a Water Saver

Earth to Student: Every time you brush your teeth, you can save water and still do a super job. Here's a chart to help you. When you brush your teeth, don't run the water unless you need it. Record your brushing here by coloring in a tooth each time you brush your teeth and save water, too.

Student's name

When your smile is colored in, add your name and pat yourself on the back!

178

The Water Works Work Sheet

Earth to Homework: You and your family can help save water, a very precious natural resource. The first step is to be aware of how much water you use each day.

Bathtub Science

1. If you have a tub/shower, fill the tub for your normal bath. Use a yardstick to measure the depth of the water in the tub. Place a piece of cloth, adhesive tape or masking tape at the height of the water. What is the depth?

   _____

2. The next day take a shower but close the drain before beginning. When your shower is done, measure the depth of the water in the tub. Is it shallower or higher than the water in the tub was?

   _____

   Which method of bathing used less water?

   _____

   Can you save water by changing your bathing habits? _____

   How many people in your family take baths each day? _____

   How many take showers each day?

   _____

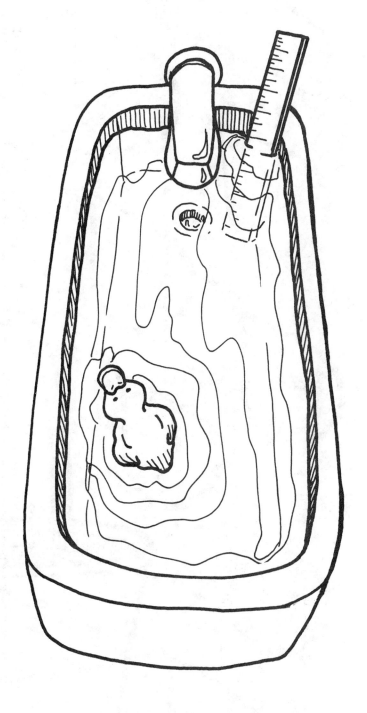

Shower Power Tip: Ask your parent if you have a low-flow shower head. Call or visit a local hardware store. Interview a salesperson, asking how much a low-flow shower head costs and how can it help save water. Also ask if there are any other ways to save water.

A low-flow shower head saves _____ gallons (liters) of water.

A low-flow shower head costs _____.

My house would need _____ shower heads costing a total of _____.

GA1342

Water Conservaton Adds Up!

Earthly Idea: Each drop of water you save adds up. Try these problems to see how much.

1 + 10 =

1 + 7 =

9 + 1 =

14 + 11 =

7 + 6 =

9 + 9 =

9 + 4 =

10 + 2 =

10 + 5 =

5 + 7 =

7 + 7 =

10 + 3 =

8 + 9 =

2 + 12 =

17 + 1 =

250 + 137 =

180

Drip, Drip, Drip

Earthly Activity: Turn on your bathroom faucet so it slowly drips. Collect the drops into a cup. Begin a timer; then answer the questions below.

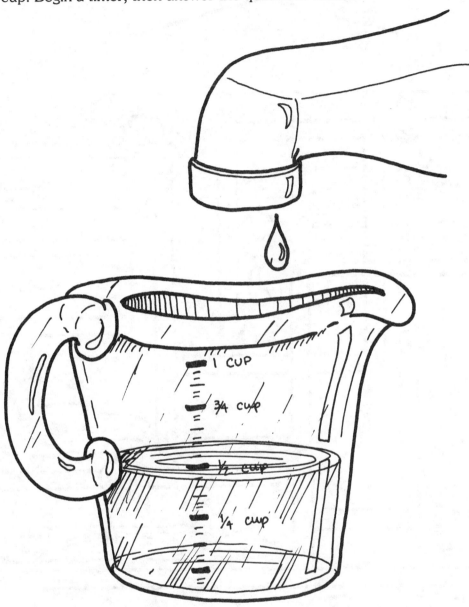

How long did it take for the cup to fill up? _____

How many faucets do you have in your house? _____

Identify the rooms that have faucets. _____

Are any of them dripping? _____

Thought Question: If every faucet in your home dripped 8 ounces (237.36 ml) of water every two hours, how many ounces (milliliters) of water would you lose a day? How many gallons (liters) of water would that add up to? _____

_____

GA1342

Fill 'er Up

Keep the water headed toward the tub. Bypass any leaks or faucets until you get to the tub.

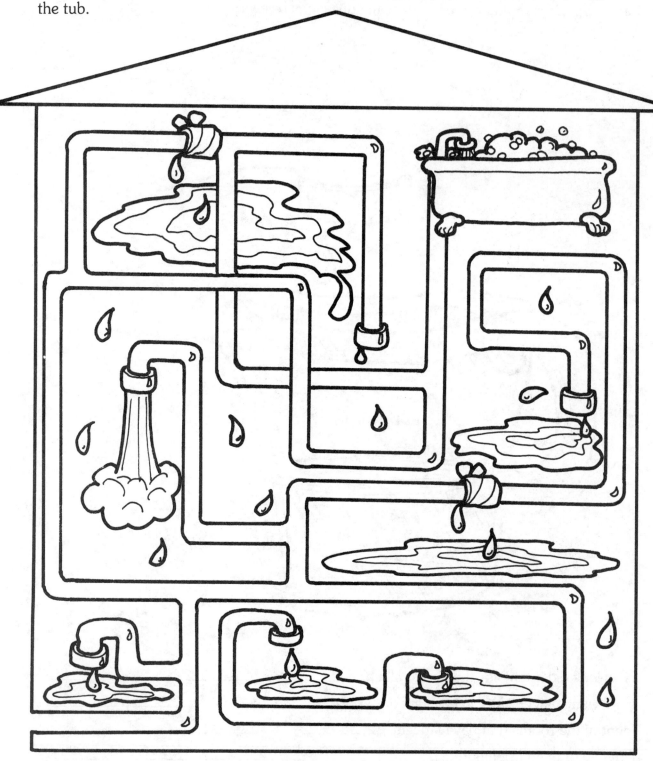

Earth Alert: Ask your Mom or Dad to help you read the water meter at your house. Turn off the water main to the house. After fifteen minutes, check the meter again. If the meter has changed, you have a leak.

GA1342

Take a Bath with Math

Water conservation adds up! Can you add these drops to find the correct answers?

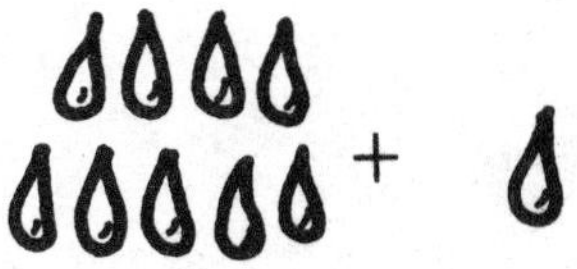

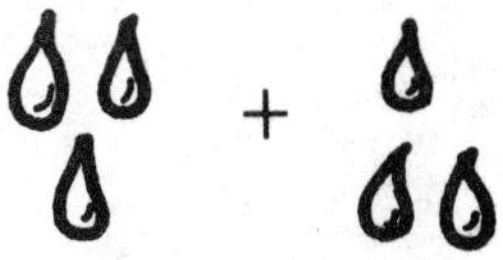

3 + 2 = _____

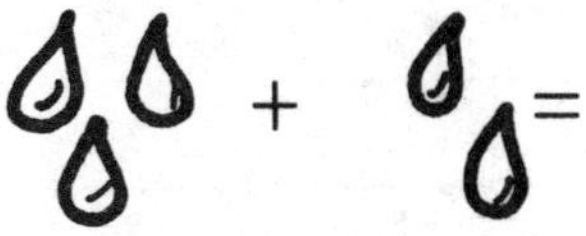

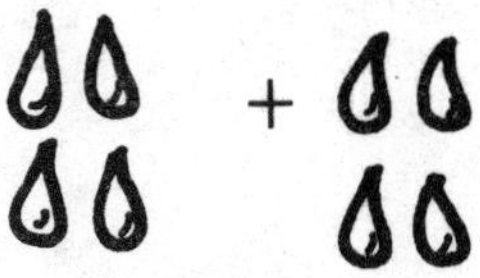

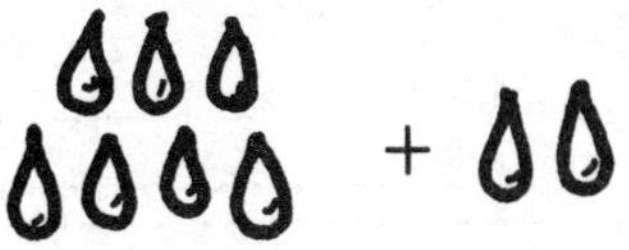

+ = _____

7 + 2 = _____

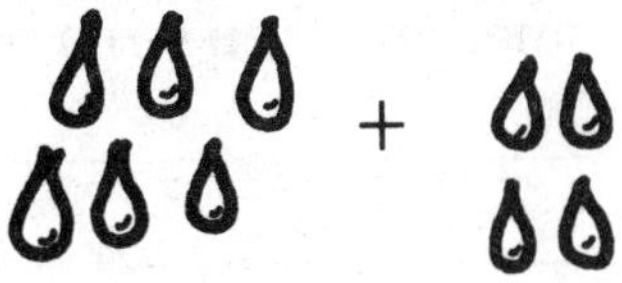

+ = _____

1 + 4 = _____

+ = _____

6 + 4 = _____

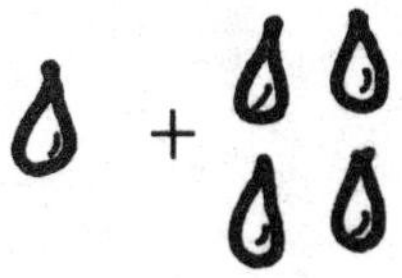

+ = _____

5 + 2 = _____

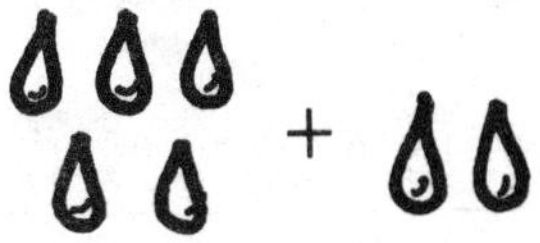

+ = _____

7 + 1 = _____

+ = _____

9 + 1 = _____

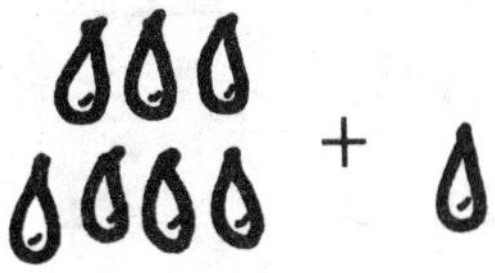

+ = _____

8 + 2 = _____

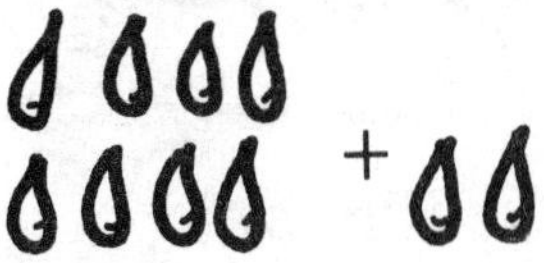

+ = _____

3 + 3 = _____

+ = _____

5 + 4 = _____

+ = _____

4 + 4 = _____

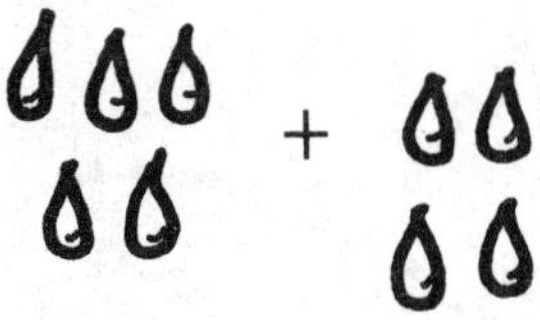

+ = _____

8 + 4 = _____

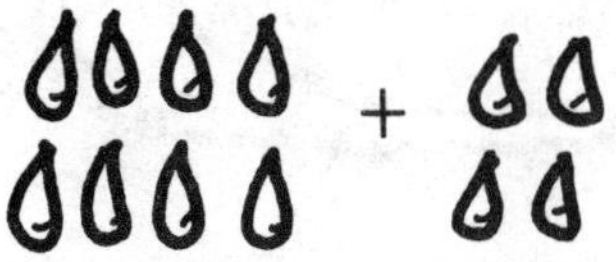

+ = _____

GA1320

Experiment H₂O

Here's a fun experiment for you to try. Collect a few rocks from outdoors. Place each one in a small glass or clear plastic jar with a lid. Fill it up halfway with water and tighten the lid. Write your name on a piece of tape and place it on your jar or jars. Try these ideas, and then record your answers.

1. How does the rock look? _____

_____

2. Let the rock sit in the jar for two days. Does the rock look different?

_____

_____

3. Shake the jar fifty times and then write down your observation.

_____

_____

4. Let the rock sit for five days. At the end of the five days, does the rock look different?

_____

_____

5. How has the water changed the rock?

_____

_____

B-Rain-Storm!

Earthly Activity: Comparing means of measuring

Materials:

straws
water
two paper cups of equal size for each child in the class
a measuring cup for each child

Procedure:

During a water break give each child a paper cup. Have each child label the cup with his name and fill the cup half full. Show each child how to put the straw in the water, place his finger over the top hole, then raise the straw and remove his finger, releasing the drops. One strawful at a time, putting each strawful in the second cup, have the student count how many drops of water are in the first cup. Record the results. After measuring with drops, have each student pour the water in the measuring cup. Record the amount poured.

Have students compare answers for each category and answer the questions below.

B-Rainstorming!

Did all of the students have the same number of drops of water?

_____

How many drops would be in a swallow?

_____

How many drops would fill a bathtub?

_____

How many drops come down in a ten-minute rainstorm?

_____

Which is the better way to measure water? Why?

_____

How much water filled the measuring cup?

_____

Which is the better way to measure water?

_____

Water Bills Add Up!

Here are your water bills. When you save water, you also help to cut down monthly expenses. Add up the totals to find how much this family spent.

Yearly: _____

What is the monthly average? _____

Which month was the highest? _____

Which month was the lowest? _____

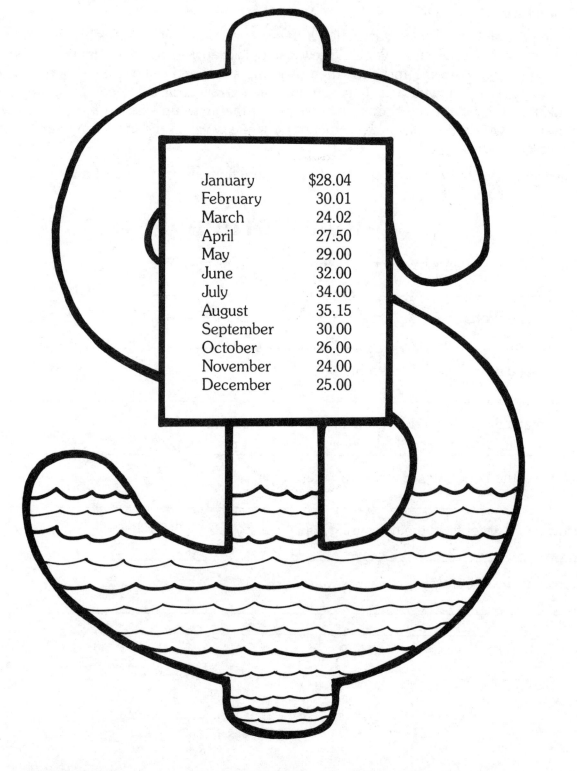

January	$28.04
February	30.01
March	24.02
April	27.50
May	29.00
June	32.00
July	34.00
August	35.15
September	30.00
October	26.00
November	24.00
December	25.00

GA1342

Good to the Last Drop!

Help save every drop of water that you can. Here are some ideas to help get you started.

Take shorter showers.

Do not use the toilet as a trash can!

Turn off the water while brushing your teeth.

Replace washers on faucets often.

How can you save water?

Scrape dishes well instead of rinsing them under running water.

How can you help?

How can you reuse water?

Be a water saver! How can you help?

Put your idea here!

Have you helped to save any water today?

GA1342

Water, Water

A cinquain poem is a very short poem. It has only eleven words.

Here's a cinquain poem about planet Earth.

Line 1: one-word title
Line 2: two words describing the title
Line 3: three words describing action
Line 4: four words telling a feeling
Line 5: one-word synonym for title

Earth
Giant sphere
Turning, speeding, pulsating
Our majestic, unique planet
Home

Earthly Activity: Write a cinquain poem about water.

Pick one of the topics below or make up your own.

Water Wasting
Drip Drop
Wet, Wet Water
The Ocean in Motion

Fill in your poem here.

GA1342

Raindrops Keep Falling!

Measure the amount of rain falling at the next rain. Place a wide-mouth jar outside on a flat surface. On a piece of masking tape draw a ruler to scale. See how much water falls and record it on this page. Compare your results with your classmates'.

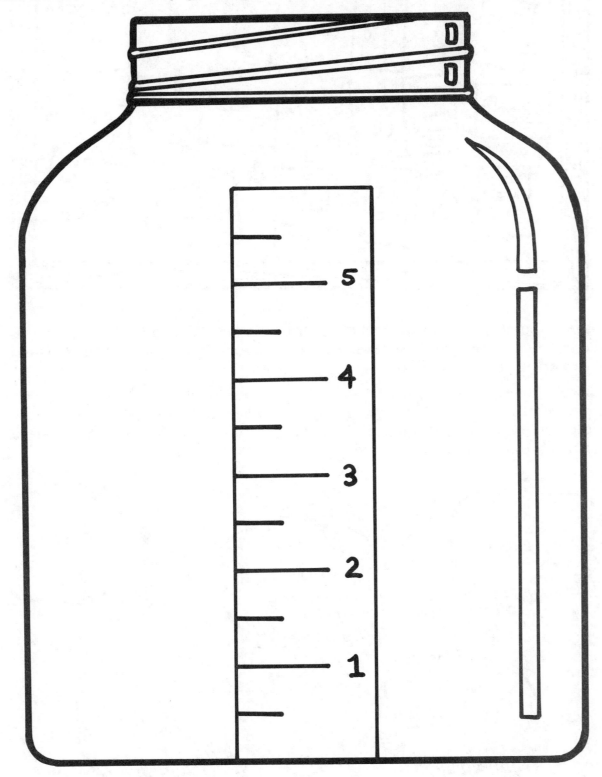

Rain, Rain, Don't Go Away!

Use this bulletin board to teach students how rain helps the earth. Let students use the title "Rain, Rain, Don't Go Away" and write poems or reports about rain. Display their work on the bulletin board.

Earthly Ideas: On a rainy day, encourage your class to talk about where rain comes from. What happens to rain? Where does rain collect after it stops and how does it disappear? Here are some rainy day words to look up in the dictionary. Students can illustrate a picture of each.

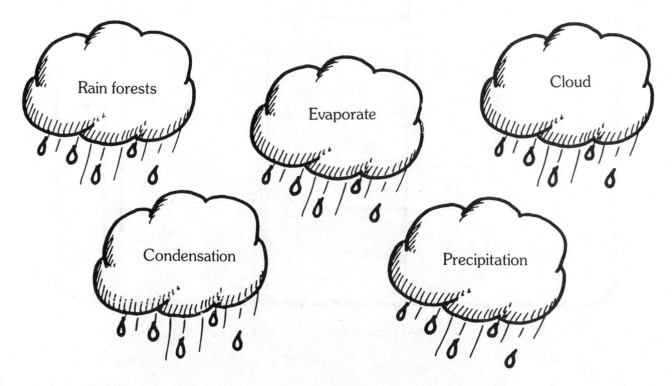

GA1342

"To Fetch a Pail of Water"

If there were no water anywhere, what do you think Jack and Jill would do? Write a story about their experience.

_____

_____

_____

_____

_____

_____

_____

_____

_____

_____

_____

_____

_____

_____

_____

_____

_____

GA1342

What on Earth You Can Do in

March

192

Earth Words for

 March

Endangered Species: These are animals facing the threat of extinction.

Rare Species: An animal of which there are very few left in the world

Threatened Species: A type of animal that may be abundant in some area but threatened by man or the environment

Extinct: An animal which no longer lives on earth

Rain Forest: An area of the earth which is very hot and very humid year 'round so that plants grow profusely

Desert: A very dry, hot area of the earth

Grassland: An area of the earth which has few trees but many grassy plains and open areas

Climate: The general weather conditions of an area

Habitat: The kind of place where an animal or plant naturally lives

Can you unscramble the words below?

thabAit _____

mileAcT _____

Dragslans _____

rear _____

tExTcin _____

streeD _____

esCieps _____

GA1342

Find Me a Home Where the Rain Forests Roam...

Count out these animals, and place them at home in the rain forest.

Species Specification

Wildlife conservationists use three classifications to identify animals and plants that are in danger of extinction.

Endangered species face the most serious threat. For example, there are only about fifty California condors alive today.

Threatened species may be plentiful in some places but threatened by man or the environment.

Rare species have small populations and live in protected environments like wildlife preserves.

What is your favorite animal? _____

It may be hard to imagine, but someday your favorite animal might be threatened. Draw a picture of your favorite animal and write a story about the world without it.

GA1342

Counting Counts

Earthly Idea: Environmentalists tag endangered species so they can count how many of the animals survive. It is very important to keep an accurate count so we know whether plans to save the animals and encourage them to have babies is working.

Earthly Activity: You are an environmentalist counting your favorite kind of animal. What kind will you count? _____

Draw a picture of your animal below.

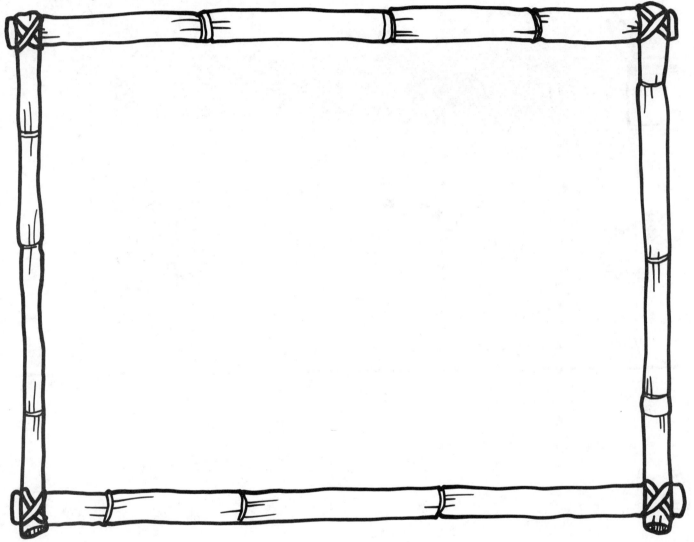

Look at the pairs of numbers below. Circle the bigger number in each pair. Watch out for the zero.

100 or 60	1000 or 10	10,000 or 999
010 or 01	101 or 111	1000 or 10,100
1010 or 10,000	100,000 or 900,000	1000 or 01100
10,000 or 9566	222,999 or 999,999	1,000,000 or 000001
1,000,000 or 11,111	001 or 101	10,000 or 01000
11,000,000 or 1,000,000,000	1,000,000,000 or 1,000,000,000	

Once upon a Time

Once upon a time, many, many thousands of years ago, the woolly mammoth roamed the earth. When the climate changed, this animal became extinct. Here is a rebus message from this animal. Can you read it?

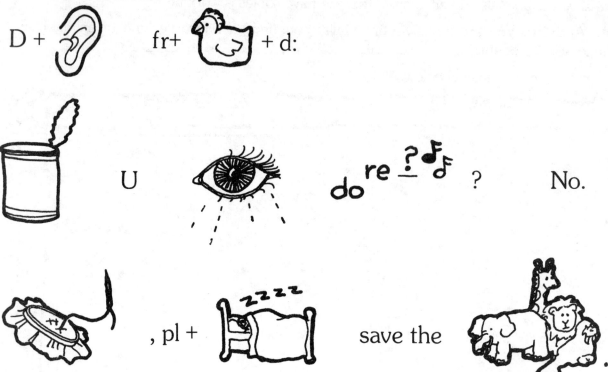

D + 🦻   fr + 🐔 + d:

🥫   U   👁   do re ♪ ?   No.

✂ , pl + 🛏   save the 🦁

Write your own rebus message below.

GA1342

Marching Right Along

There are all kinds of animals on earth. They come in all shapes and sizes and live in all parts of the world. So far scientists have identified about 1,000,000 kinds of animals, but new ones are discovered every year. Unfortunately, some animals have become extinct so they no longer live on earth.

Draw a parade of animals. Beginning with the letter *A* and continuing to *Z*, see if you can march along with an animal for each letter.

A is for alligator.
B is for bear.
Here are a few animals to get you there.

GA1342

Lifesavers

Earthly Idea: Since 1600 many animals have become extinct. In North America the Carolina parakeet, the passenger pigeon, the California grizzly bear and the Florida black wolf have all become extinct. Beginning in the late 1800's, people have become increasingly concerned about vanishing wildlife. Setting aside national parkland and passing laws to protect threatened species have helped save some animals. The American bison and Florida alligators were saved by such efforts.

There are many species that are still in danger. The great elephant is being killed for its ivory. The Asiatic lion, the Bengal tiger, the blue whale, the orangutan, the mountain gorilla, the whooping crane, the California condor and the Asian rhinoceros each face extinction.

Earthly Activity: Select an endangered species to study. Write a paragraph about what the earth will miss if this animal becomes extinct.

On the day there are no more _____,

_____

_____

_____

_____

_____

_____

_____

_____

_____

_____

_____

_____

_____

GA1342

Ode to a Dying Species

Choose an endangered species from the list below or one that you know about. Write a poem about the animal. The form below is called a diamante poem because the shape of the poem is a diamond.

Elephant
Leopard
Sea turtle
Eagle

Noun
Adjective, Adjective
Participle, Participle, Participle
Noun, Noun, Noun, Noun
Participle, Participle, Participle
Adjective, Adjective
Noun

Eagle
Proud, strong
Soaring, sailing, flying
Emblem, symbol, hero, bird
Fleeting, scrounging, dying
Wild, rare
Species

GA1342

Animals at Home

Animals live everywhere on earth. They live in the air, in the ocean and in all kinds of climates. Usually the animals in a location have lived there for thousands of years so they have adapted to the surroundings.

The grasslands are large areas of open countryside. Most of the fastest animals live in these areas. So do some very large animals. Animals that live in the grasslands include elephants, hippopotamuses and rhinoceros. Swift runners include ostriches and zebras. Lions and giraffes live in the grasslands of Africa. The kangaroo lives in the grasslands of Australia.

Look on the world map below. The shaded areas show where the grasslands of the world are. Can you name some of these areas? _____

_____

How many continents have grasslands? _____

Can you name some of the countries that have grasslands?

_____

_____

_____

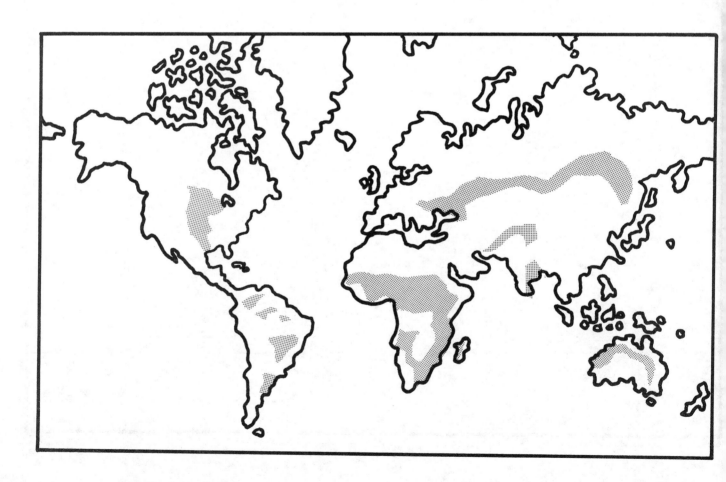

GA1342

Make a Match

Endangered animals live all over the world. Can you match where these animals come from? Draw a line to connect the animal with its home.

Polar bear   South America

Orangutan   South America

Galápagos tortoise   Malaysia

Spectacled bear   Arctic

Asiatic lion   Asia

Bald eagle   Australia

Kangaroo   America

Antelope   Africa

Leopard   Asia

GA1342

Home, Home on the Rain Forests

The rain forests have a climate that stays hot all year long. In the tropical rain forests, the tops of the trees and vines form a thick overhead covering called a canopy. The monkeys play in the canopy. Orangutans, gibbons and other apes live in the rain forests. Colorful parrots and other birds live in the trees. Snakes and insects grow to a very large size in the rain forest environment and roam the entire forest.

Color the rain forest below. Cut out the animals on the next page and place them where they will be happy in the rain forest.

202

Find Me a Home
Where the Rain Forests Roam . . .

Cut out these animals and place them at home in the rain forest on page 202.

GA1342

Habitat Sweet Habitat

A habitat is a place where an animal or plant naturally lives and also grows. Four habitats that are very important are the ocean, desert, wetland and rain forest. Draw animals and plants that live in each.

Rain Forest	Desert
Wetland	Ocean

GA1342

Endangered Animals

The sea turtle is an endangered species. The sea turtle's shell protects him; however you can help protect this endangered species and others, too. Research the sea turtle or another endangered animal and write a report.

Where's My Home?

Each animal has a particular type of habitat or home that suits it best. One reason animals become threatened is that their home territory is changed by man or changes in the environment. The rain forests in South America are being cut down at the rate of 100 acres (40 ha) a day. As the human population grows, people take over lands where animals used to live. If the animals cannot find a safe, new home that fits their needs, they may not survive.

Choose from the list in the box to identify where each of these animals prefers to live.

grasslands	polar regions
forests	desert
oceans	rain forests
mountains	

goat _____   coyote _____

giraffe _____   camel _____

elephant _____   penguin _____

squirrel _____   snowy owl _____

beaver _____   octopus _____

monkey _____   whale _____

tarantula _____

Endangered Species

Some animals like dinosaurs and mammoths became extinct naturally. Other animals become extinct because they are hunted or their habitats are destroyed by man.

In 1973 Congress passed the Endangered Species Act which provides better protection for threatened and endangered species of wildlife. The act prohibits any acts that would harm the habitat of an endangered species, although in 1978 Congress excluded certain projects from this law.

Since 1600 many kinds of animals have become extinct or endangered. Look up one of these animals in the encyclopedia to find out what happened to it.

Carolina parakeet

Florida black wolf

Passenger pigeon

California grizzly bear

Whooping crane

Asian rhinoceros

California condor

Mountain gorilla

One way to protect animals is to place them in wildlife preserves where hunting is outlawed, and the animals are protected by law. Is there a game preserve near you? Is there a bird sanctuary in your town?

GA1342

Tale of an Endangered Species

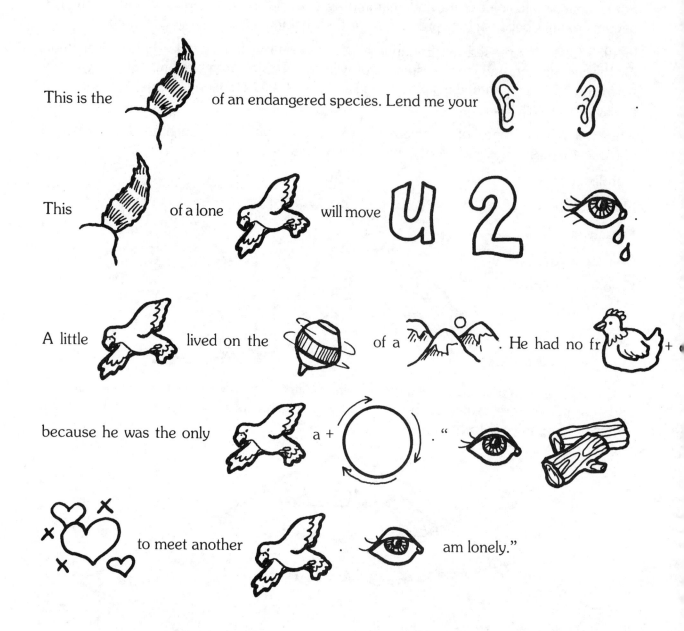

This is the [shell] of an endangered species. Lend me your [ear] [ear].

This [shell] of a lone [dove] will move u 2 [eye/tear].

A little [eagle] lived on the [top] of a [mountain]. He had no fr[hen]+

because he was the only [eagle] a + [circle/round] . " [eye] [log]

[hearts] to meet another [dove] . [eye] am lonely."

How can the little bald eagle make some friends? Use all the social skills you know to tell your story. To make a rebus, substitute pictures for words wherever you can.

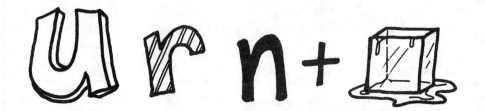

GA1342

Catch Me If You Can

One of the ways animals protect themselves from predators, animals that might eat them, is with camouflage. Often an animal will have some features that make it look like its environment. Find a chameleon, a leopard and a hyena in the picture below. Then look up these animals in the encyclopedia to find out what kind of protection nature has given them.

Earth Alert: What kind of protection do animals have against man?

_____

_____

_____

_____

GA1342

Monkey See, Monkey Do . . . .
This Monkey Needs a Home, Too!

This little monkey lost his home when the jungle was cut down to make room for a road. He has nowhere to go. Help him find the rest of his family and a new tree to live in.

Start

210

GA1342

Materially Speaking

Earthly Activity: Many of the things we eat, wear or use in our everyday lives are made of parts of animals or plants. Other items are man-made or made from synthetic fibers made by man.

Put each item below in the correct category. Is it animal, plant or synthetic? What else can you add to the list?

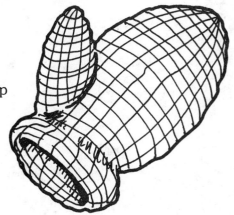

steak
leather shoes
hair ribbons
plastic barretts
paper
books
sheets
wool sweater
T-shirt
cereal

doll
model car
grapes
raisins
chocolate syrup
mittens
wallet
hose
silk dress
pencil

Item	Natural Material	Synthetic

GA1342

Who "Nose"?

Can you identify which nose belongs to each animal? Put a heart on each endangered species once its nose is in place.

212

GA1342

Baby Animals

Unlike you, some young animals need very little care from their parents. Others rely on their parents to feed and protect them until they can take care of themselves.

Sea urchin and starfish parents pay no attention to their young. Ants and bees take very special care of their young as do many birds and mammals. Kangaroo keep newborn babies in a pouch on the front of the mothers' bodies.

Look at each row below. Can you fill in the row so it includes the name of the baby, its mother or father and the kind of animal it is.

Animal	Parent	Young
		kitten
	dog	
goat	billy	
		fawn
turkey		poult
bobcat		kit
fox	vixen	
goose		gosling
	stallion	colt
		chick
lion		
hog		

GA1342

Earth to Worms

Earthworms are very helpful animals that live in the soil. After a rain they come out of the soil for air. Go outside after a rain and search the earth for earthworms. Answer these questions after you find one.

Where did you see the earthworm? _____

What was it doing? _____

How did it move? _____

Be kind to earthworms. They are good for the soil; they help make it rich!

GA134

What Bugs You?

Earth to Student: On each bug write something that "bugs" you about the way your fellow earthlings treat planet Earth. How about things that need to be improved around home and school? The first step in problem solving is identifying the problem.

GA1342

Give a Bug a Break

Earth to Student: When it is possible, give a bug a break and return it to the outdoors. Some bugs are poisonous or may sting you, so ask a grown-up to identify the insects you see. Many household insecticides have ingredients that are harmful to the environment. Ask your parents how they get rid of unwanted bugs.

Many insects are very helpful to the environment. Can you find out what kind of helpful jobs each of these insects has?

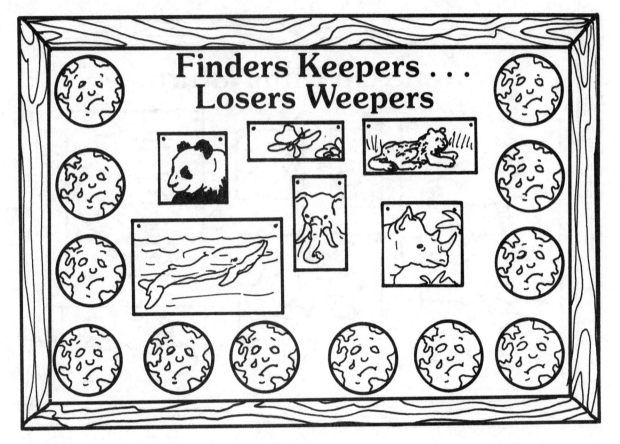

Finders Keepers . . .
Losers Weepers

Use this bulletin board to highlight the tragedy of endangered species. Once a species vanishes from earth, it is gone forever. Border the bulletin board using the pattern with a tearful planet Earth below. Decorate the board with pictures of endangered species.

Have students write cinquain poems using the instructions below about the animals they would miss the most and why.

Line 1: one-word title   _____
Line 2: two words describing the title   _____ _____
Line 3: three words describing action
Line 4: four words telling a feeling   _____, _____, _____
Line 5: one-word synonym for title   _____ _____ ____ _____

                                                      _____

GA1342

Tone Up with Nature

Inspire students to focus on physical fitness. Have a classroom discussion about how animals exercise. What do we do that they do, too? Students can illustrate their ideas, and you can display them on the board.

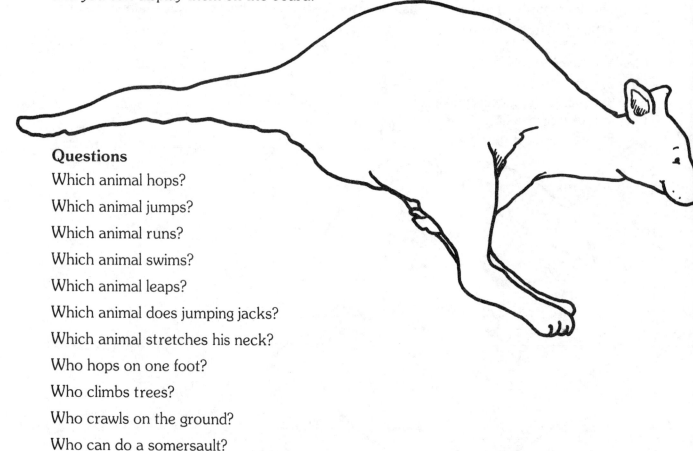

Questions

Which animal hops?

Which animal jumps?

Which animal runs?

Which animal swims?

Which animal leaps?

Which animal does jumping jacks?

Which animal stretches his neck?

Who hops on one foot?

Who climbs trees?

Who crawls on the ground?

Who can do a somersault?

218

GA1342

Tales of Nature

Use this bulletin board to inspire a creative writing unit. Instruct each student to choose an animal that has a tail and to write a "tale" about the animals from the shapes below and add their artwork next to their tales of nature.

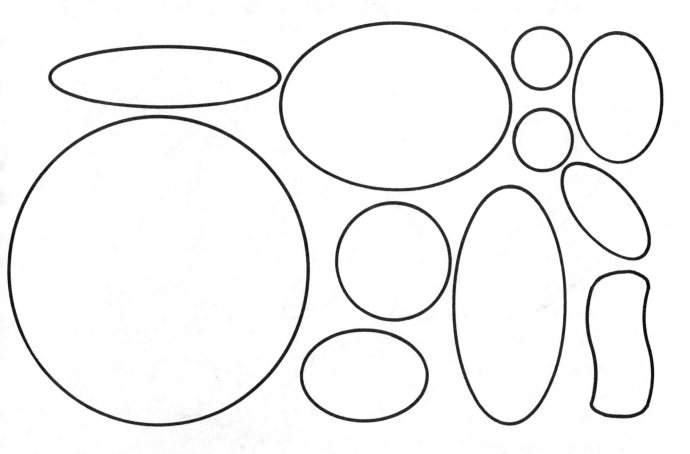

Birds of a Feather Work Together

Use this "fine feathered" bulletin board to encourage class cooperation while focusing on birds during the winter season. Duplicate a bird for each student and put it on the board with his name on it. Each time he helps another student, thinks of someone else or cooperates give him a feather to add to his bird. This is also the ideal unit to pay attention to our fine feathered friends—birds. Give each student a *Bird*'s the Word work sheet on page 84 and add them to the display for a new idea.

Student's name

220

GA134

Endangered Zoo

ZOO

Create a drawing of your own zoo. All the animals included must be endangered species.

GA1342

Home Sweet Home

Earth to Homework: Many acres of rain forest are being cut down every year to clear land for ranching. The animals who live in the rain forests are being forced to find new homes.

Many fast food restaurants buy beef from cattle ranchers who raise cattle on these lands. Call the fast food restaurants in your area. What is the source of their meat?

In the space below, compose a letter that you would use to convince someone not to cut down the rain forests.

_____

_____

_____

_____

Dear _____ :

_____

_____

_____

_____

_____

_____

_____

_____

_____

Sincerely,

_____

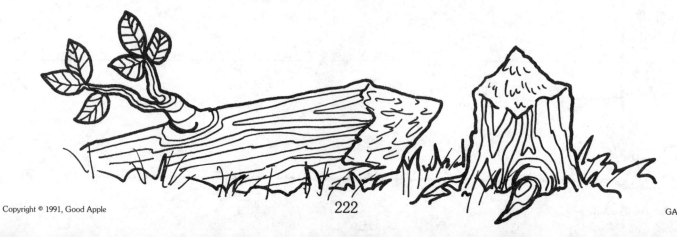

GA1342

Going, Going, Gone

Endangered animals are animals that are in danger of becoming extinct. When an animal is extinct, it is gone forever. Today's endangered animals are in trouble mostly because of people. How do you think you can help animals? Write your ideas here.

_____

_____

_____

_____

_____

_____

_____

_____

_____

_____

_____

_____

_____

_____

_____

_____

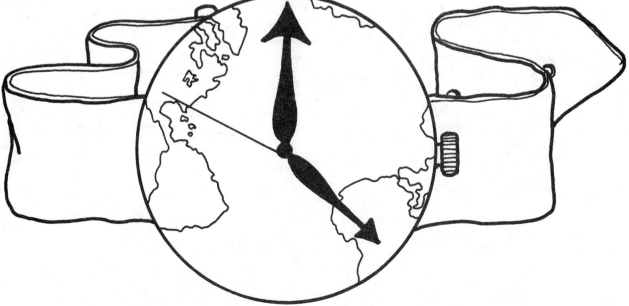

GA1342

What on Earth You Can Do in

April

224

Earth Words for

April

Atmosphere: The air surrounding the earth and extending up to 1000 miles (1610 km) above the earth

Ionosphere: The outer region of the atmosphere beginning beyond the stratosphere

Stratosphere: The region of the atmosphere beyond the troposphere and beneath the ionosphere

Troposphere: The lowest part of the atmosphere where the clouds float

Thermosphere: The atmosphere has five layers: the troposphere (up to 10.5 miles [16.9 km]), the stratosphere (up to 31 miles [49.91 km]), mesosphere (up to 53 miles [85.33 km]), the thermosphere or ionosphere (up to 310 miles [499.10 km]) and the exosphere (above 310 miles [499.10 km]).

Igneous Rock: Rocks formed when melted rock deep inside the crust cools and hardens

Sedimentary Rock: Rocks developed from material worn away from the land by water and wind

Metamorphic Rock: Rocks formed from chemical changes to sedimentary and igneous rocks

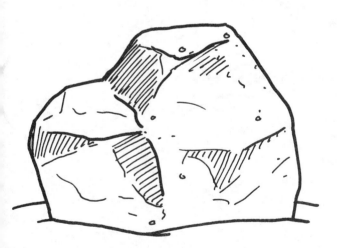

Continent: Continents are part of the rocky skin of the earth. Land masses separated by water

Circumference: The distance around a circular area

Diameter: The distance through a circular area

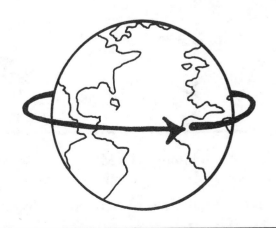

GA1342

Earth Is It

The earth seems very big to us, but it is only a very small part of the universe. The earth may be small in the universe, but it is the home of man and many living things. No one has found life on any other planet in our galaxy, the Milky Way.

Living things can survive on earth because it is just the right distance from the sun. We need the sun's light and warmth. If the earth were too close to the sun, it would be too hot, and if the earth were too far from the sun, it would be too cold for living things.

Can you find the earth in the map of the solar system? Label the planets: Mercury, Pluto, Earth, Mars, Saturn, Jupiter, Venus, Uranus and Neptune.

Earth to Homework: Make up a sentence that will help you remember the order of the planets from the earth to the sun.

Hint: Start each word with the first letter of the planets in order from the sun.

Home Is It!

We think that earth is a very big place. How big is it?

The earth is 24,901.55 miles (40,091.495 km) around at the equator.

The circumference or distance around the earth through North and South Poles is 24,859.82 miles (40,024.31 km).

The earth weighs 6,600,000,000,000,000,000,000 tons. (That is 6.6 sextillion.)

The earth is 93,000,000 miles (149,730,000 km) from the sun.

The surface of the earth is approximately 30 percent land, 70 percent water.

The distance through the earth at the equator is 7926 miles (12,760.86 km).

On the map of the earth below, label the dimensions. Is the earth perfectly round?

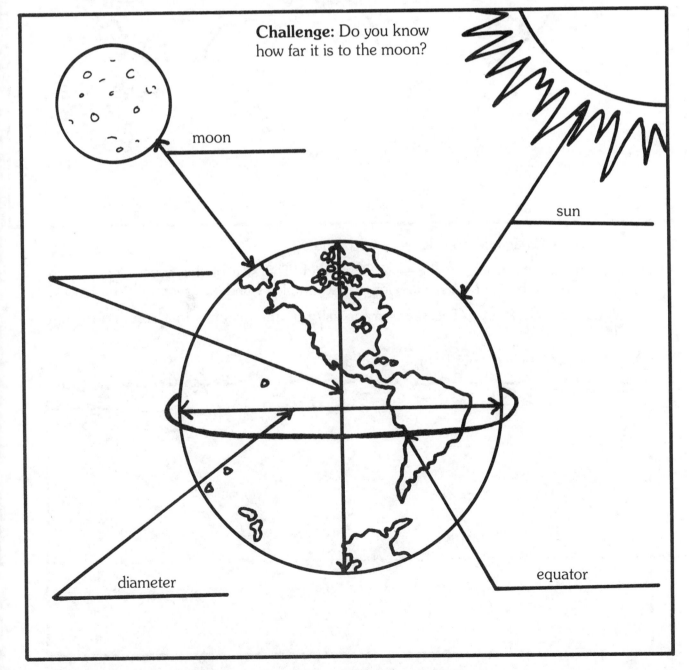

Challenge: Do you know how far it is to the moon?

moon

sun

diameter

equator

GA1342

The Earth Is "All" Wet!

Not quite. The total area of the earth's surface is 196.949 square miles (510.09 sq. km). Approximately 70 percent of the earth's surface is covered by oceans.

Look at the map below. List the names of all the oceans on the earth.

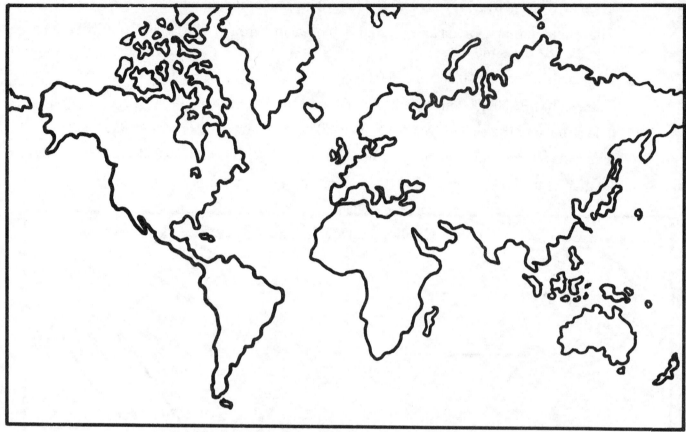

Here are some ocean questions to ask your friends.

1. What makes the waves in the sea? (The wind. The size of the waves depends on the size of the body of water, how long the wind blows and how fast the wind blows.)

2. Why is seawater salty? (The sea is made salty by the minerals that run into it from rivers.)

Draw a picture below of your favorite ocean activity.

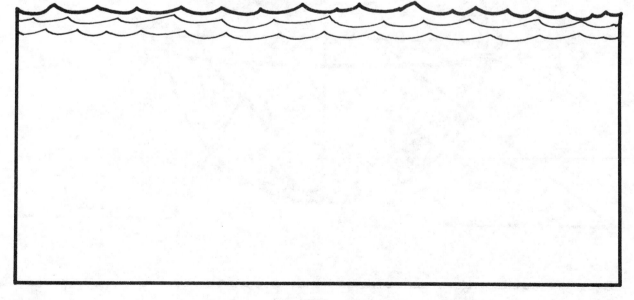

GA1342

Know Your Continents

More than 200 million years ago all the land masses on earth were joined. That supercontinent was called Pangaea. About 100 million years ago, Pangaea began to break into pieces forming the continents we know today.

Look at the map below.

Color Africa brown.
Color Eurasia blue.
Color Australia green.

Color North America red.
Color South America yellow.
Color Antarctica orange.

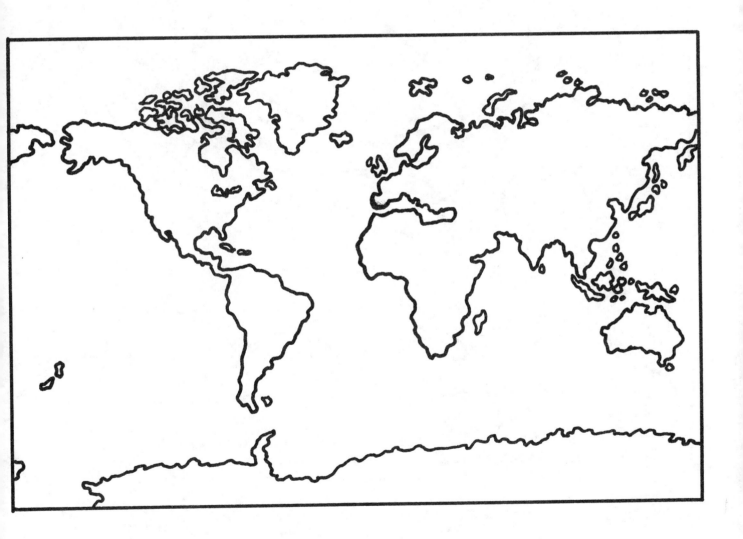

GA1342

It's All Relative

How big is big?

The earth is 24,901 miles (40,090.61 km) around at the equator. 1 mile (1.61 km) = 5280 feet (1605.12 m).

Use a ruler to measure the circumference around your classroom. How many feet (meters) is it around your classroom?

Earth Alert: How many times would you have to walk around your classroom to walk a mile (kilometer)?

How many times would you have to walk around your classroom to walk the same distance as the circumference of the earth?

GA1342

Let's Rock It!

Let's take a closer look at rocks. Rocks come in many different shapes, colors and sizes. Collect twelve rocks and observe their differences and similarities. Record your observations here.

Colors of my rocks: _____

_____

_____

How do they differ in size? _____

_____

_____

How do they differ in texture? _____

_____

_____

Draw the shapes of your rocks here.

GA1342

Taking Rocks for "Granite"

A rock is a mass of mineral matter. Did you know the earth's crust is composed of rock? There are three major kinds of rocks. They are sedimentary rocks, igneous rocks and metamorphic rocks. Look up these words in the dictionary and find the answers to the questions.

What is a sedimentary rock? _____

_____

_____

_____

_____

Sedimentary rocks are used to make cement, glass, _____, _____ and _____.

What is an igneous rock? _____

_____

_____

_____

_____

What is a metamorphic rock? _____

_____

_____

_____

_____

_____

GA1342

Earth Watch

Solve the riddles and find the answers in the puzzle below. Circle the words and fill in the blanks.

An animal that climbs and swings in the rain forest ___ ___ ___ ___ ___ ___

Three quarters of the earth is covered in this. ___ ___ ___ ___ ___

To reuse a product ___ ___ ___ ___ ___ ___ ___

Cans that can be recycled are made of this. ___ ___ ___ ___ ___ ___ ___ ___

Trash ___ ___ ___ ___ ___ ___ ___

Our planet ___ ___ ___ ___ ___

Chemicals that kill bugs and pests ___ ___ ___ ___ ___ ___ ___ ___ ___ ___

A mixture of decaying organic material ___ ___ ___ ___ ___ ___ ___

Dirt in the air ___ ___ ___ ___ ___ ___ ___ ___ ___

Buying things that can be recycled ___ ___ ___ ___ ___ ___ ___ ___ ___

A place where trash is disposed of ___ ___ ___ ___ ___ ___ ___ ___

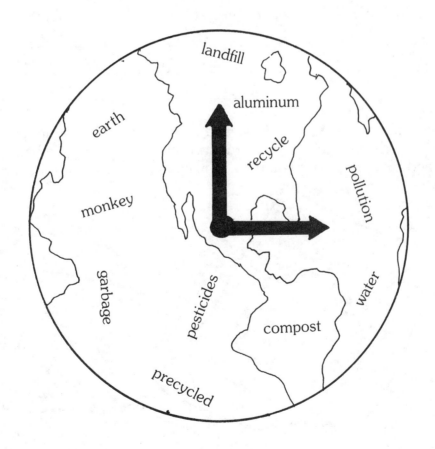

233

GA1342

Solid as a Rock!

Join the pack; be a rock hound.

Many people enjoy collecting rocks. It may seem hard to identify rocks at first, but after a while it becomes quite easy. You may buy an inexpensive starter kit that will help you identify common rocks and minerals. Rock hobbyists enjoy trading their rocks.

To begin a rock collection, you need some rocks. In your yard find three rocks; then answer these questions about each rock.

Where did you find the rock? _____

_____

_____

Sedimentary rocks usually lie in layered formations. They often contain fossils and have markings made by water. Igneous rocks are usually solid and crystalline. Metamorphic rocks usually have bands that make it easy to split them into sheets or slabs.

What happens when you pour soda pop on the rock? _____

_____

_____

There are many chemical tests that can be done to identify rocks. A simple test is to pour some soda pop over the rock. If the pop fizzes, then the rock specimen has limestone in it.

Scrape the rock across a hard, rough surface like concrete. What color is the streak that is made? _____

_____

_____

Clean your rock with soap and water and a stiff brush. Catalogue the rock by painting a small identifying number on it. In a record book write the number, where you found the rock and the kind of rock you think it might be.

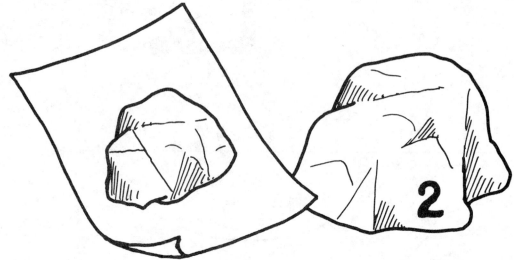

GA1342

What Is Under You?

There is always rock under you. The skin of the earth is called the *crust*. The crust is 5 miles (8.05 km) deep in some places and 20 miles (32.2 km) deep in others.

The crust of the earth is made of three kinds of rock.

Igneous: Rocks formed when melted rock inside the earth hardened

Sedimentary: Rocks developed from material that collected and hardened as the earth was worn away by wind and water. This rock contains many pieces of other things like shells and bones.

Metamorphic: Rocks that are formed from igneous and sedimentary rock by chemical processes, heat and pressure

Use the dictionary or encyclopedia to identify what kind of rocks the following ones are.

granite _____

_____

_____

quartz _____

_____

_____

sandstone _____

_____

_____

marble _____

_____

_____

flint _____

_____

_____

shale _____

_____

_____

pumice _____

_____

_____

GA1342

Story Starters

Earth to Student: Help finish this story and bring it back to earth. Happy landing!

Once upon a time a _____ landed on planet Earth. When _____ got out

of his _____, he looked around and _____

_____

_____

_____

_____

_____

_____

_____

_____

_____

_____

_____

_____

_____

_____

_____

_____

_____

_____

GA1342

April Flowers Need April Showers

Observe the flowers near your house. How do they look before and after a rain? Why is the rain important? Draw your flower garden here.

GA1342

Planter Pizzazz

Each container can be recycled into beautiful planters for growing seeds or repotting plants. Students can collect milk cartons, old pots and a variety of containers. Use this page to inspire ideas, and then have an EARTH project where students make their own planters.

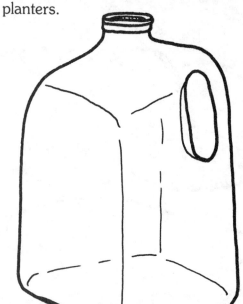

Can you recycle a plastic carton?

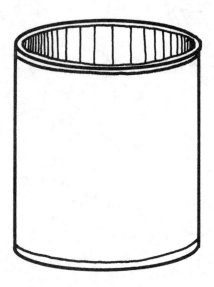

What could you do to a can?

How can you jazz up an old clay pot?

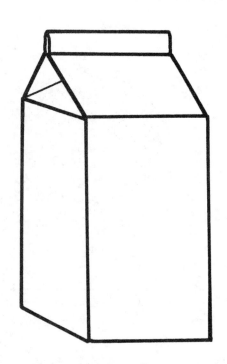

How can you recycle a milk carton?

GA1342

It Takes Two!

Some jobs take two people to do. Name some jobs that take two people. (For example, washing and drying dishes)

_____

_____

_____

Find a partner. As a dynamic duo, suggest three jobs you can do to:

1. Beautify your classroom
2. Clean up the school
3. Save a piece of planet Earth

Write your plans here.

_____

_____

_____

_____

_____

_____

_____

_____

_____

GA1342

Seven Wonders of the World

In ancient times the Greeks and Romans would make lists of memorable things that people should see. All the lists the Greeks and Romans made included only man-made objects.

The Seven Wonders of the Ancient World are

The Pyramids of Egypt

The Hanging Gardens of Babylon

The Temple of Artemis in Greece

The Statue of Zeus in Greece

The Mausoleum in Turkey

The Colossus of Rhodes

The Lighthouse of Alexandria

World travelers and explorers consider Mount Everest, the Grand Canyon and the Great Barrier Reef of Australia to be some of the wonders of the natural world.

Pretend you are going to take a trip around the world. Where would you go? _____

_____

_____

What would be the seven wonders of the world you would want to see? _____

_____

_____

Make an itinerary for your trip.

GA1342

You-nique!

There's only one you.

There is only one earth. It is special. How is the earth different from all the other planets?

_____

_____

How is the earth like all the other planets? _____

_____

You are special, too. You are unique. There is no one else in the whole world just like you. Use the graph below to discover the ways you and your classmates are alike and different.

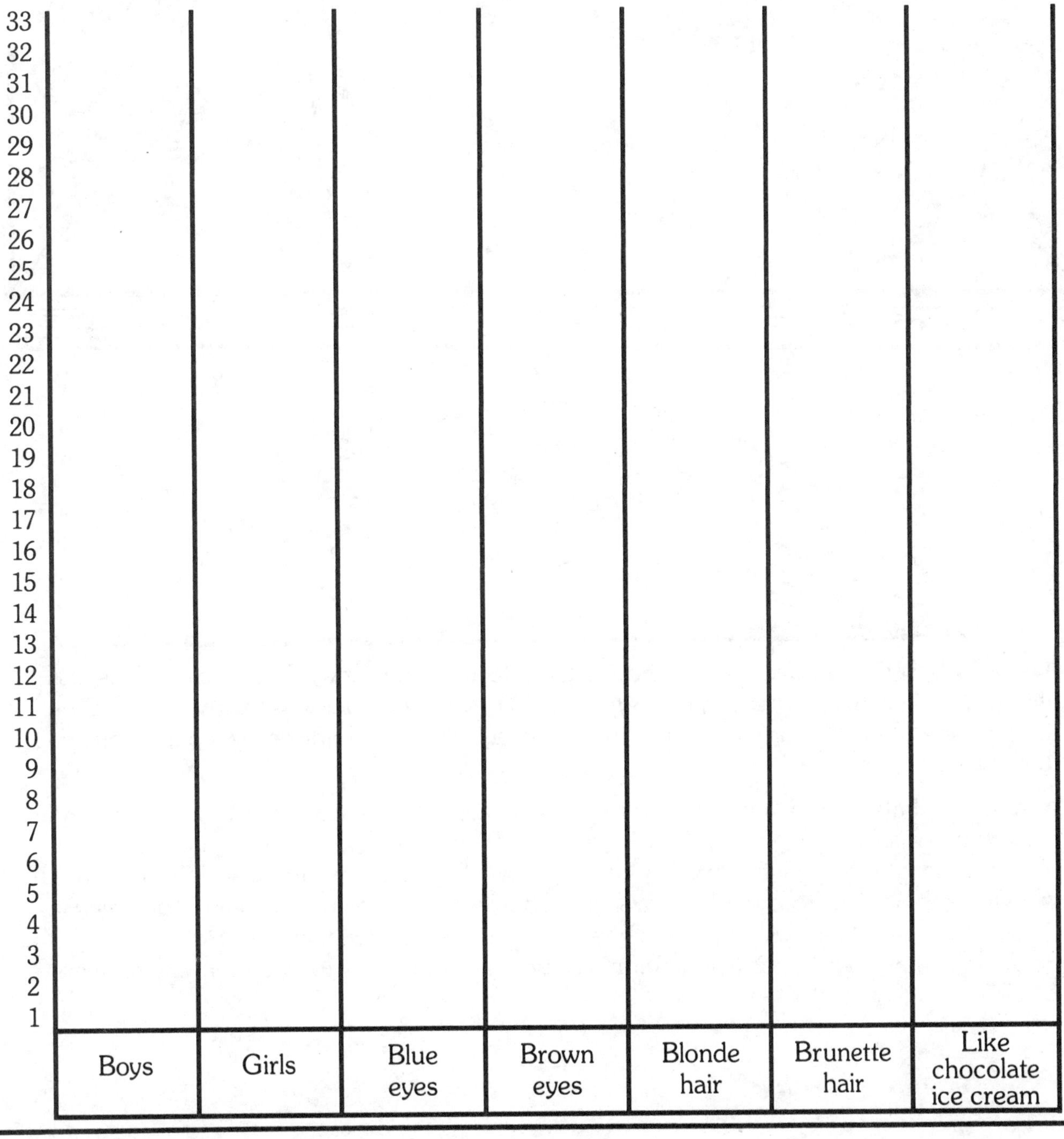

	Boys	Girls	Blue eyes	Brown eyes	Blonde hair	Brunette hair	Like chocolate ice cream
33							
32							
31							
30							
29							
28							
27							
26							
25							
24							
23							
22							
21							
20							
19							
18							
17							
16							
15							
14							
13							
12							
11							
10							
9							
8							
7							
6							
5							
4							
3							
2							
1							

Don't Make a Scene . . .
Keep the Earth Clean!

Use this bulletin board to encourage students to keep the environment clean. Discuss with the class what would happen to the earth if everyone littered. What would happen if everyone kept it clean? Try some of the ideas below to reinforce keeping America beautiful.

- Cleanup Patrol: Appoint a group of students each week to patrol assigned areas and pick up trash.
- Make signs to help keep America beautiful and display them throughout your school.
- Ask each student to choose an area to adopt with his family and clean it up weekly. Compare results each week to see how your students are helping the earth.
- Write a thank-you letter to a community worker who helps to keep the environment clean.

GA1342

Where Is the Ozone Layer?

The earth is surrounded by a layer of gases called the *atmosphere*. Gravity keeps the atmosphere close to earth. Five hundred miles (805 km) above the earth's surface the air is very thin.

The atmosphere has five main layers.
Look at the drawing below. Label each area. Use the scale to measure the mileage on the illustration.

The troposphere is about 10.5 miles (16.9 km) high. This is where most of the earth's weather occurs.
The stratosphere goes up to 31 miles (49.91 km). It contains most of the atmosphere's ozone. Ozone absorbs the dangerous ultraviolet rays of the sun.
The mesosphere goes up to 53 miles (85.33 km).
The thermosphere goes up to 310 miles (499.10 km).
The topmost layer is called the ionosphere.

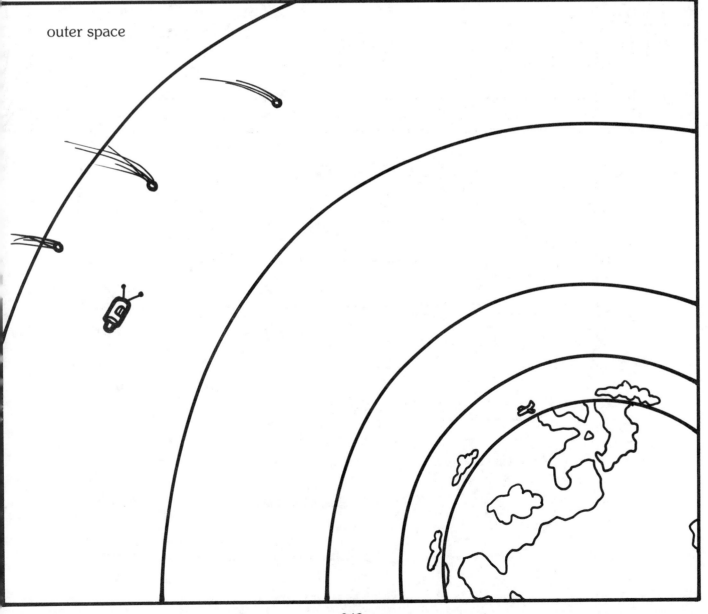

outer space

GA1342

Some"Bunny" Loves the Earth!

A petition is a formally drawn up request addressed to an authority soliciting a favor or request for a cause. Decide what you think needs to be done to help the earth. Write a statement of your request.

Ask your friends, neighbors, etc., to support you by signing their names to show they agree.

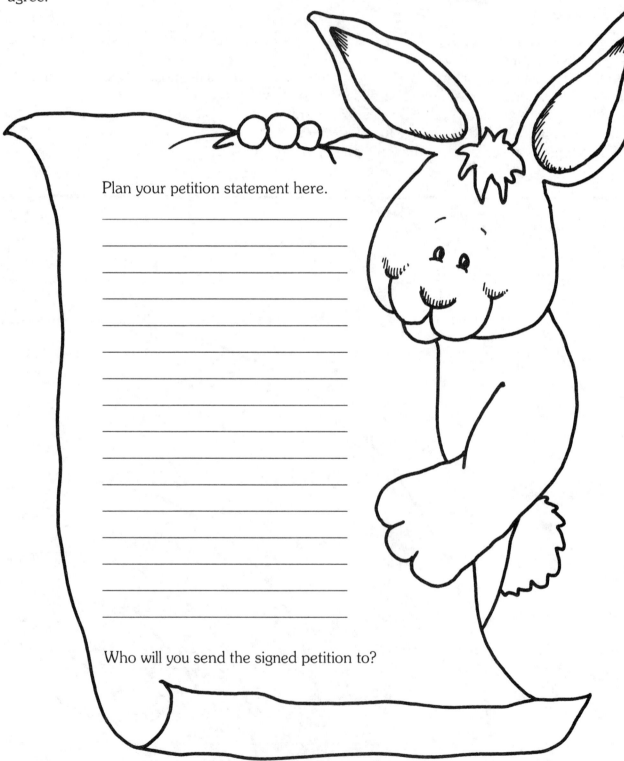

Plan your petition statement here.

_____

_____

_____

_____

_____

_____

_____

_____

_____

_____

_____

_____

_____

_____

Who will you send the signed petition to?

Petition

Statement of Purpose: _____

_____

_____

_____

We the undersigned agree with the above statement and ask the authority to consider our statement.

	Name	**Address**
1.		
2.		
3.		
4.		
5.		
6.		
7.		
8.		
9.		
10.		
11.		
12.		
13.		
14.		
15.		
16.		
17.		
18.		
19.		
20.		
21.		
22.		
23.		
24.		
25.		

Give a Hand to Mother Earth

Everyone likes a compliment. Mother Earth likes to be appreciated also. Another way we pay a compliment to Mother Earth is by taking care of her. On each finger below, write one thing you should remember to do to take care of Mother Earth.

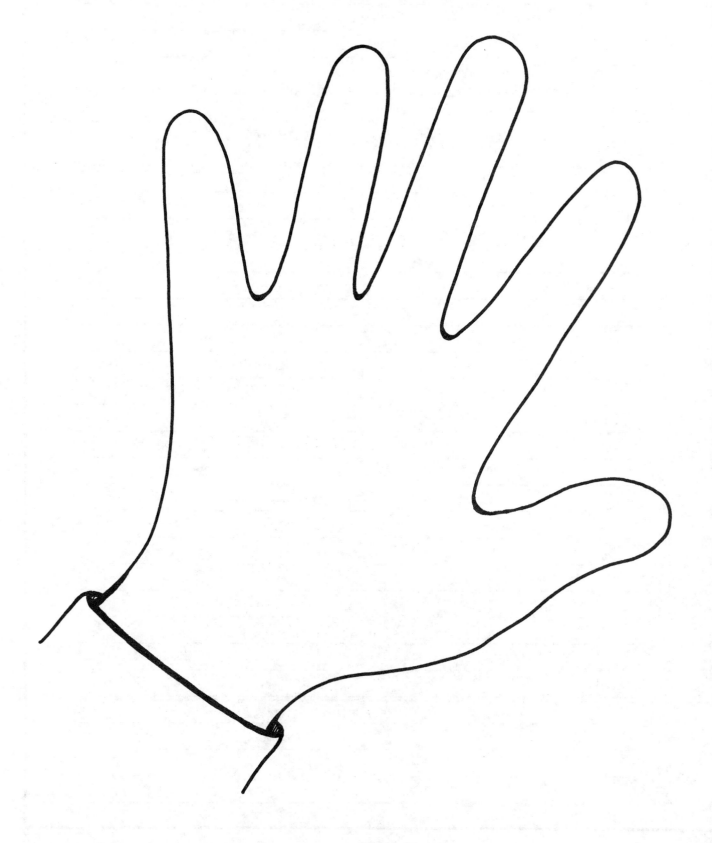

Have You Heard the Word?

See how many words you can find that begin with the same letter as these words:

earth: earthling, earthly, _____

_____

recycle _____

_____

environment _____

_____

litter _____

_____

pollution _____

_____

garbage _____

_____

energy _____

_____

help _____

_____

GA1342

Reading Is out of This World!

This is your record sheet. Every time you read a library book, your spaceship reaches a star, so color it in. When you reach planet Earth, you are home and can color the entire picture!

248

GA1342

The Earth's Wish List

Help make a wish list for things the earth might need.

1.

2.

3.

4.

5.

6.

7.

8.

9.

10.

What are some things you can get your family to do? _____

_____

What can you do? _____

_____

_____

_____

GA1342

Cover Up

You are the author of a new book all about helping planet Earth. Design your cover here.

GA1342

All Eyes on Nature

Go outside and observe your front yard or a wooded area for five minutes. Then come inside and draw a picture of everything you saw.

GA1342

Opposite Ends of the Earth

Can you match each word with its opposite? Draw a line to connect the correct pairs.

hot	awake
up	old
big	short
sleepy	cold
new	sad
tall	run
happy	little
walk	down
fast	sour
sweet	quiet
loud	soft
hard	slow
closed	open

GA1342

"Sun"sational

When the sun is shining, it sends light and heat energy to the earth. Draw pictures of all the things that the sun's energy helps.

GA1342

Down to Earth Feelings

Use this bulletin board to encourage students to write their feelings in the form of poems. Display the poems on the board. Here are some titles for the poems.

I Love the Earth
Litter Loser
Cash for Trash
Ready, Set, Recycle
Energy Energize
I Can Help

Earthlings, Listen
Go, Go, Garbage
Going, Going, Gone

GA1342

What on Earth You Can Do in

May

GA1342

Earth Words for May

Global Warming: One of the most dangerous problems facing the earth. Global warming is the general warming of the planet's climate because of the depletion of the ozone layer that protects the earth from the rays of the sun.

Ozone: A natural gas made of three oxygen atoms. The ozone layer in the atmosphere protects the earth from harmful ultraviolet radiation.

Greenhouse Effect: A common term for the warming of the earth's climate. The phenomenon occurs because of the absorption of solar radiation and its effects on the earth's environment so that the earth's average temperature is warming.

Ultraviolet Radiation: A type of radiation emanating from the sun's rays that can be harmful to man, animals, plant life and the environment

Acid: A large class of substances which can turn litmus paper red and are capable of dissolving certain kinds of metals. It is sour to the taste.

Alkaline: A bitter substance that has a pH greater than 7 and contains the chemical substance that is alkali

Phosphates: A classification of chemicals often used in detergents which do not break down for disposal easily

Climatologist: Person who studies the weather and its patterns

Match the term to its clue word.

bitter	climatologist
soap	phosphate
sour	ultraviolet
sun	greenhouse effect
warming	ozone
atmospheric condition	acid
oxygen	global warming
weather	alkaline

GA1342

Hot News About Global Warming

SAVE THE ELEPHANTS
DOWN WITH PAPER TOWELS
RECYCLE TIN CANS
RIDE YOUR BIKE
PLANT A TREE
REUSE GLASS BOTTLES
SAVE WATER
STOP DRIPS AND LEAKS
TURN THE HEAT DOWN
RECYCLE YOUR NEWSPAPER
DON'T RELEASE HELIUM BALLOONS

Cover a bulletin board with old newspaper. Have the students trace the "fire" pattern on red, yellow and orange construction paper and write a relevant slogan on each. Ask each student to select a topic—Global Warming, Acid Rain, Destruction of the Rain Forests, Endangered Species, etc., and write a letter stating his or her position to the local congressman. Post the letters on the bulletin board before sending them.

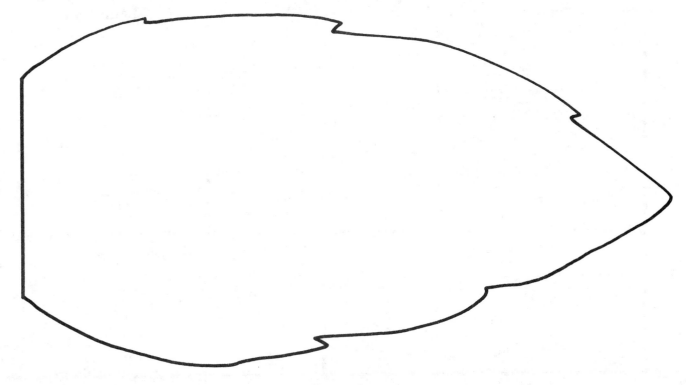

GA1342

Global Warming—It's No Joke

Global warming is one of the biggest threats to our planet. During this century man has released a huge amount of "greenhouse gases" into the environment. Greenhouse gases include *carbon dioxide, methane, chlorofluorocarbons, nitrous oxide* and other gases that create ozone. The burning of *fossil fuels* produces greenhouse gases. Fossil fuels are coal, oil, gas and wood.

Deforestation also produces these gases. Chlorofluorcarbons are used in refrigerators, air conditioners and aerosol cans. These account for 17 percent of the greenhouse effect.

In each room of the house list the aerosol cans you find that use chlorofluorocarbons. Can you and your family think of substitutes?

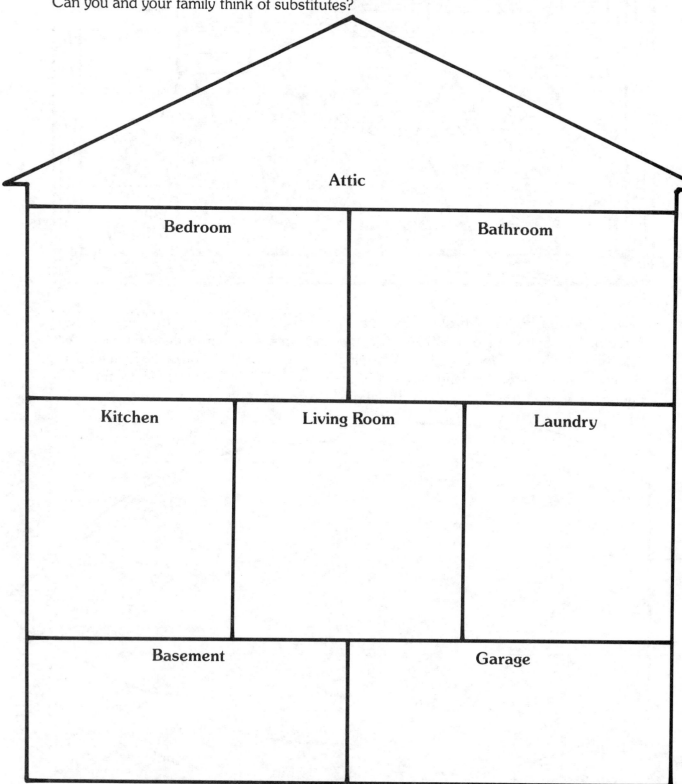

Attic

Bedroom

Bathroom

Kitchen

Living Room

Laundry

Basement

Garage

GA1342

Average Up!

Global temperature is higher today than it was in 1862 which was the first year climate was measured. Record high temperatures have been reached *five* times in the 1980's: in 1980, 1981, 1983, 1987, 1988.

Climatologists predict that the summers will be even hotter in the 1990's. Answer these questions about the chart below.

What was the average temperature on Monday? _____

Which week had the highest average high temperature? _____

Which date had the lowest temperature? _____

Which week had the most rainfall? _____

Week 1	M	T	W	Th	F	S	S
High Temp.	88	86	90	85	91	90	89
Low Temp.	55	65	68	65	64	65	66
Rainfall	.02	.00	.5	1.00	.00	.00	.00
Week 2	M	T	W	Th	F	S	S
High Temp.	80	83	85	80	86	86	85
Low Temp.	60	58	58	62	60	59	60
Rainfall	.50	.50	.11	.00	.00	.00	.00

GA1342

 Danger Endangered Species

Can you imagine never seeing another kitten? Another elephant? A tortoise? Not all of these animals are endangered species, but they could be.

Design a poster that tells people not to buy ivory products or tortoise shell products. Hunters kill elephants for their tusks and tortoises for their shells.

To receive a complete list of endangered species, write:
    The Office of Endangered Species
    Fish and Wildlife Service
    U.S. Department of the Interior
    Washington, D.C.

GA1342

Earth-a-Bet

Earth to Student: Below each letter write an environmental word that begins with it.

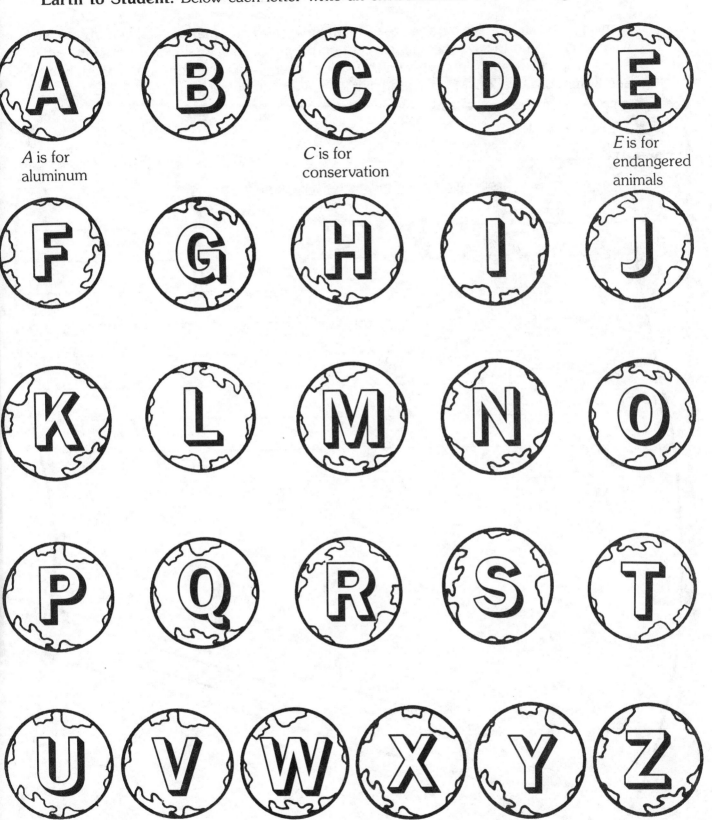

A is for
aluminum

C is for
conservation

E is for
endangered
animals

What You Can Do

Convince a friend to take better care of earth or write a letter to Mom and Dad suggesting what they can do to save the environment and prevent additional global warming. What have you learned about global warming, recycling, energy conservation, endangered species and water conservation. Make strong opinion statements to get your point across.

Dear _____,

The earth has a problem and that means we have a problem. . .

_____

_____

_____

_____

_____

_____

_____

_____

_____

_____

GA1342

"Ooh, It's Getting Warm Out Here!

Scientists have already detected an average rise in temperature of 1^0 F ($.55^0$ C). They predict a continued rise of 4 to 9^0 F (2.22 to 5^0 C). by the middle of the twenty-first century.

In the chart below record the low and high temperatures each day. Then add 9^0 F (5^0 C) to each extreme to predict the temperature in the year 2050. What do you think the weather will be like?

Day	Low Temp.	High Temp.	Low Year 2050	High Year 2050
1				
2				
3				
4				
5				
6				
7				
8				
9				
10				
11				
12				
13				
14				

GA1342

Rain, Rain, Come This Way

Have you ever wondered how the weatherman knows how much it has rained? Put a bucket outside your back door. Tape a measuring stick to the side. For two weeks measure how much rain fell during the twenty-four-hour period. Compare the amount you measure with how much rainfall the weatherman says occurred.

Day	Rainfall at Home	Weatherman	Difference

Wrap It Up

The earth has an envelope of air around it. About 7 to 15 miles (11.27 to 24.15 km) above the surface of the earth is a layer of *ozone* which is made of *3* oxygen atoms bound together. The ozone layer is very important. Ozone is the only gas that acts as a "natural sunscreen" screening out much of the ultraviolet radiation from the sun.

Man needs the ozone layer to save him from the dangerous rays of the sun. Draw pictures of other things that protect human beings from harm.

GA1342

Time Out for Summer

With summer approaching, encourage your students to make time to help the earth during vacation time. Ask each student what makes him tick? How can he or she help save the earth's treasures? Duplicate the clock and add each student's name. Students can write their timely ideas for helping on the clocks and display them on the board.

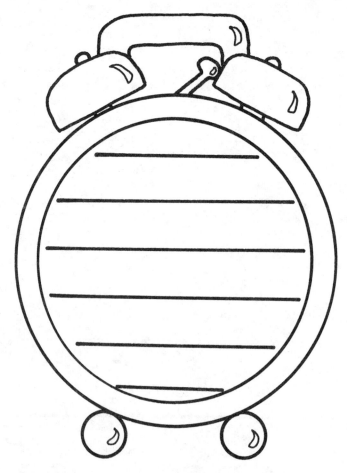

266

GA1342

Some Sun Safety

The ozone layer helps protect us from some of the sun's dangerous ultraviolet rays. It acts like a "natural sunscreen."

Ultraviolet B rays can damage DNA and hurt crops and animals. Some ultraviolet radiation hurts skin and causes wrinkles. It may even cause skin cancer.

How should you protect yourself when you are out in the sun? Draw protective clothing on the child below. And don't forget the sun screen!

GA1342

Weather or Not . . . Here We Come

There's always the weather to talk about. Watch the weather report each day. Record the day's high and low in the chart below. What was the previous low or high temperature for the date? Did the weather set any new records during the week? Was the weather sunny, cloudy or rainy?

Day	High Temp.	Low Temp.	Record High	Record Low	Weather
Monday					
Tuesday					
Wednesday					
Thursday					
Friday					
Saturday					
Sunday					
Average for Days					

GA1342

Look What I "Can" Do

Earth to Student: List all the things you "can" do to help keep the earth clean and keep the earth healthy. Post your list at home.

1. _____
2. _____
3. _____
4. _____
5. _____
6. _____
7. _____
8. _____
9. _____
10. _____

GA1342

Rhyme It—Write It!

List all the words you can think of that rhyme with each word below. (If you don't think of a rhyming word, write a synonym and *circle* it.)

can   trash   globe   light

recycle   litter   walk   tree

oil   endangered   energy

GA1342

Recycling Survey

Here is a survey to ask your friends and relatives. Write the answers to the questions and compare your answers with your classmates'.

		Yes	No
1.	Do you recycle?	____	____
2.	If so, do you recyle		
	aluminum cans	____	____
	grocery bags	____	____
	newspapers	____	____
	magazines	____	____
	plastic bottles	____	____
	plastic containers	____	____
	glass bottles and jars	____	____
3.	Do you need help recycling?	____	____
4.	Do you think recycling is important? Why?	____	____

GA1342

Look at Yourself . . . What's on Your Shelf?

This symbol ♻ means "packaged in recycled materials." Search your pantry. Which of the items come in recycled packaging? Next time Mom or Dad goes grocery shopping, check each item for this symbol.

_____ milk carton

_____ cereal box

_____ soup can

_____ detergent box

_____ egg carton

_____ scouring pads

_____ bottled drinks

_____ canned drinks

_____ diapers

_____ cookie box

_____ glass jars

_____ wax paper

FIZZ

COOKIES

EGGS

100% RECYCLED CARDBOARD

WAX PAPER

SOUP

CEREAL

100 PAPER PLATE

TOMATOES

POP

GA1342

Battery Alert

How many objects in your house use batteries? Add up the batteries by kind and number. More than 2,000,000,000 batteries are sold in the U.S. each year. The chemicals in throw-away batteries are sometimes very toxic. When they are thrown away they can leak into the soil.

Object	Size and Number of Batteries Needed				
	AAA	AA	A	C	D

Earth to Homework: How much does your family spend on batteries each year? Estimate the total. How could your family save money and help the earth?

GA1342

An Acidic Assignment

At the hardware store or pet store you can buy litmus paper strips to test how acidic water is. The litmus paper will also come with a color chart. If you compare the color the litmus paper turns to the color on the color chart, you can determine whether a substance is acidic or alkaline. pH values measure acidity and alkalinity. A pH of 7 is right in the middle—the substance is neither acidic nor alkaline.

Dip a piece of litmus paper in each substance below. What is its pH? Is it acid, alkaline or neither? Mark the chart appropriately.

Substance	pH	Acid	Alkaline	Neither
rainwater				
lemon juice				
Coke				
milk				
tap water				

Earth to Homework: Which cities in the United States have the worst acid rain problem? Which cities have the most industry?

GA1342

The Helpful Hand Award

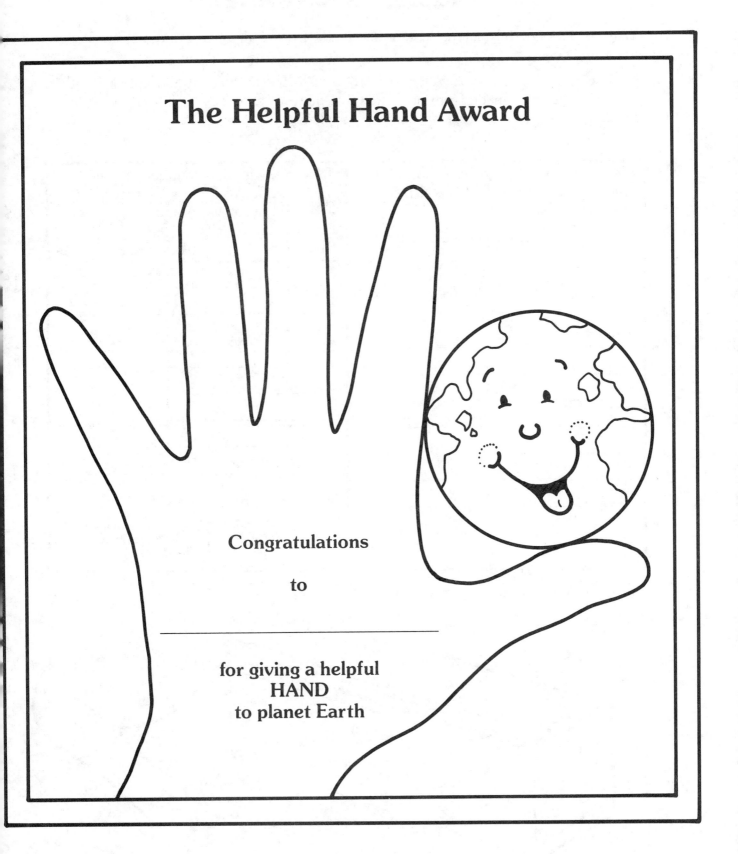

Congratulations

to

_____

**for giving a helpful
HAND
to planet Earth**

GA1342

Plastic Is a Waste!

Plastic is a wonderful material chemically made from a number of natural substances like oil and coal.

Plastic can be hard or soft, pliable or strong. It keeps food fresh and is sturdier than glass. *But* plastic is made from nonrenewable natural resources, and it is very difficult to recycle and takes hundreds of years to decompose.

On a trip to the grocery store, list everything you find that has a plastic wrapper or package.	Take a walk around your house. What's made out of plastic? Don't forget nylon and vinyl, clear wrap and cellophane, Styrofoam.
_____	_____
_____	_____
_____	_____
_____	_____
_____	_____
_____	_____
_____	_____
_____	_____
_____	_____
_____	_____
_____	_____
_____	

Circle the items you can buy in another form.

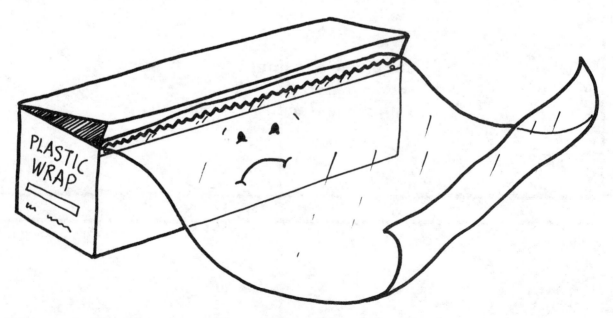

GA1342

Perfectly Packaged!

Earth to Student: Try your hand at redesigning a toy or food package. Draw a picture showing how the manufacturer did it, and then draw your idea to show how to use less materials.

For example, boxed drinks are very difficult to recycle because there is foil between the paper layers. What kind of package would be better?

Before	After
boxed drink 	
plastic milk carton 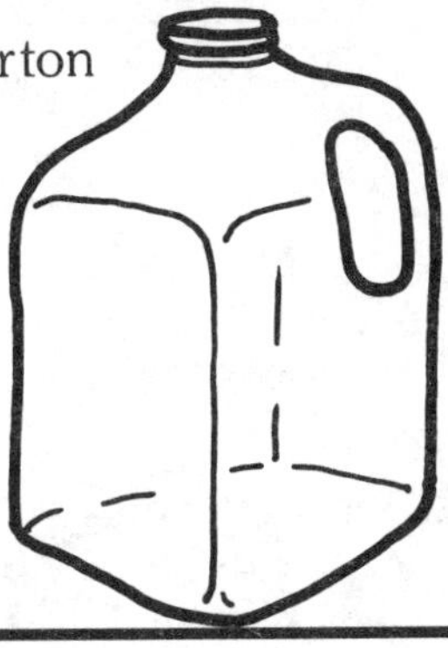	

277

GA1342

With Mom's or Dad's Help Only!

Some commercial cleaners have toxic or dangerous ingredients that might be harmful to you or dangerous to the environment.

Do the laundry detergents Mom uses have *phosphates* in them? Phosphates do not easily break down.

What kind of detergent does your family use? _____

At the grocery store, read the detergent labels to find one without phosphates.

_____

With GROWN-UP HELP, look at the chemicals and cleaners around the house. Which ones say they are dangerous?

_____   _____
_____   _____
_____   _____
_____   _____
_____   _____

278
GA1342

The Greatest Resource on Earth!

How old are you?

One of earth's greatest resources is its people.

There are a lot of people who have been on this earth much longer than you. Select two people who are much older than you to interview. The purpose of the interview is to find out how life on earth has changed since they were children.

Who will you interview? _____

_____

What questions will you ask each person? List your interview questions here.

1. _____

2. _____

3. _____

4. _____

5. _____

6. _____

What did you find out?

_____

_____

_____

_____

_____

_____

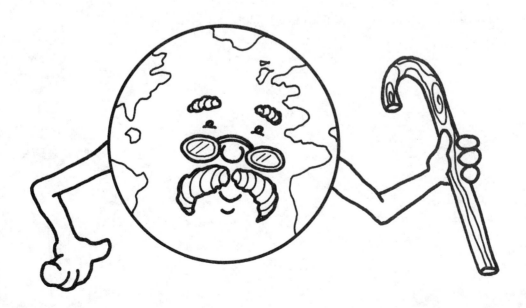

GA1342

Count on Mother Earth!

Use this bulletin board to teach students to identify and spell numerals from 1 and up! List the numerals on index cards and their correct spellings. Encourage students to do the following math activities.

1. Add up all the numbers on the bulletin board.

2. Add up all the even numbers.

3. Add up all the odd numbers.

4. Count by 2's up to 20.

5. Find your age on the board.

6. Assign a number to each letter of the alphabet—A is 1, B is 2, etc. Write a secret code birthday greeting and add it to the bulletin board.

7. How old is Mother Earth?

GA1342

Figure It Out

The greenhouse effect is causing the earth to warm. If the climate warms on the average of ½ degree each year for fifty years, how warm would it be outside today?

It takes 16,000 kilowatt-hours of electricity to produce one ton (.9 t) of aluminum from ore. It only requires 187 kilowatt-hours to make one ton (.9 t) of aluminum from recycled metal. How many kilowatt-hours of electricity do you save this way?

If every citizen in a city discards 5 pounds (2.25 kg) of trash a day and there are 2.5 million people in the city, how many pounds (kilograms) of trash are thrown away each week? How many tons (tonnes)?

If twenty-three aluminum cans weigh one pound (.45 kg), how many cans of aluminum are there in a bag of aluminum cans that weighs 5½ pounds (2.47 kg)?

GA1342

How Does Newspaper Stack Up?

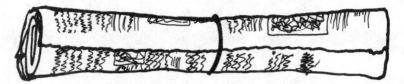

 A foot (30.48 cm) of newspapers tightly tied together weighs approximately 30 pounds (13.5 kg). Measure a stack of newspapers your family has collected. Tie together a bundle that is one foot (30.48 cm) high. How much does it weight?

 Figure out how many stacks exactly like the one you will have tied it would take to measure one ton (.9 t).

 If you stacked all of those bundles on top of each other, how tall would the stack be?

GA1342

Litter Bug Treasure Hunt

Over the next week, search for these items that would be discarded or thrown away. Divide into teams and see who can collect them all.

broken pen
used aluminum foil
plastic bottle
broken branch
plastic cup
cereal box
soda can

broken crayon
broken toy
plastic bag
paper bag
paper napkin
torn clothing
soda bottle

lunch bag
leaf
button
paper toilet roll
bottle cap
broken pencil

Earthly Idea: Sort these objects into recyclable materials and take them to a recycling center in your neighborhood.

GA1342

What Is Your Opinion?

The biggest problem we have on earth is _____

_____

_____

_____

I can help by _____

_____

_____

_____

_____

My family is helping to _____

_____

_____

_____

_____

I wonder most about _____

_____

_____

_____

_____

The biggest change I've made is _____

_____

_____

_____

_____

When I grow up I hope _____

_____

_____

_____

_____

GA1342

Step Right Up . . . and Help the Planet Earth!

Earth to Student: Get friends, neighbors and family members to sign this petition. Then send it to your mayor with a letter about why you believe in recycling.

We the undersigned believe all citizens should separate their trash into paper, glass and aluminum. The city could then easily recycle the materials and put the money earned into the city budget.

GA1342

"Fun"d Raising

P.T.A. stands for Parents and Teachers Association and is the helping organization that makes your school great. *P.T.A.* can also stand for Please Take Action or Parents Take Action. Think of ways your P.T.A. can help the environment and your school.

Write a letter to the P.T.A. president at your school suggesting a student-parent-teacher project that's good for the earth.

Dear _____:

_____

_____

_____

_____

_____

_____

_____

_____

_____

_____

Sincerely,

_____

GA1342

"Sun"sational Kid

_____

student's name

is a
shining example
of
an earth helper!
Hoo"ray,"
Hoo"ray"!

_____

parent or teacher's name

287

GA1342

What on Earth You Can Do with Kids

During Vacation

Earth Day, Every Day

Earth Day is a special day that encourages others to think about helping the earth. It occurs during April and is a wonderful celebration for the ever-deserving earth. Make a sign which helps others remember Earth Day.

Lend Your Reach and Save the Beach!

Earth to Student: If you plan to visit the beach this summer, you can help save the beach. Every day trash is being thrown on the beach. This litters the ground and can wash into the ocean and harm the fish and creatures in the sea. Here are some tips to remember.

Don't throw plastic bags or plastic six-pack rings away. A fish could get caught.

If a beach toy breaks, bring it in. Do not leave its parts on the beach.

Don't throw cans on the beach. Bring a reusable thermos to drink from.

Bring along a cloth or reusable beach bag. Leave plastic bags at home.

When the tide washes in, make sure you've cleaned up your beach toys. They could wash out to sea!

If you picnic at the beach, bring your trash back to your home. Don't leave it on the beach. Recycle what you can!

Bring along a trash bag and see how much trash you can pick up. Just think . . . your reach could save a fish and save the beach!

Earth to Student: How can you help?

Grocery Bingo

When you go shopping at the grocery store, see how many foods you can find or items that are listed on this bingo card. Cross them off as you find them. Decide which ones use too much packaging and which ones do not.

B	I	N	G	O
Package that uses too many wrappers	Food not in a wrapper or package	Food with two wrappings	Food with a foil cover	Food in a tray in a bag
Cookies in a bag in a box	Food in a plastic tray in a bag		Food not in a wrapper or package	Cookies in a box
Bread in a plastic bag	Food in a box	Food in a jar	Organically grown food not in a wrapper	Food in a plastic container
Food without a wrapper		Meal in a plastic container	Cardboard container	Cereal in a bag in a box
Plastic grocery bag	Food in two wrappers	Recyclable grocery bag	Food without a wrapper	

Recycling Roundup

Here are the basic steps for recycling. Draw a picture of each one.

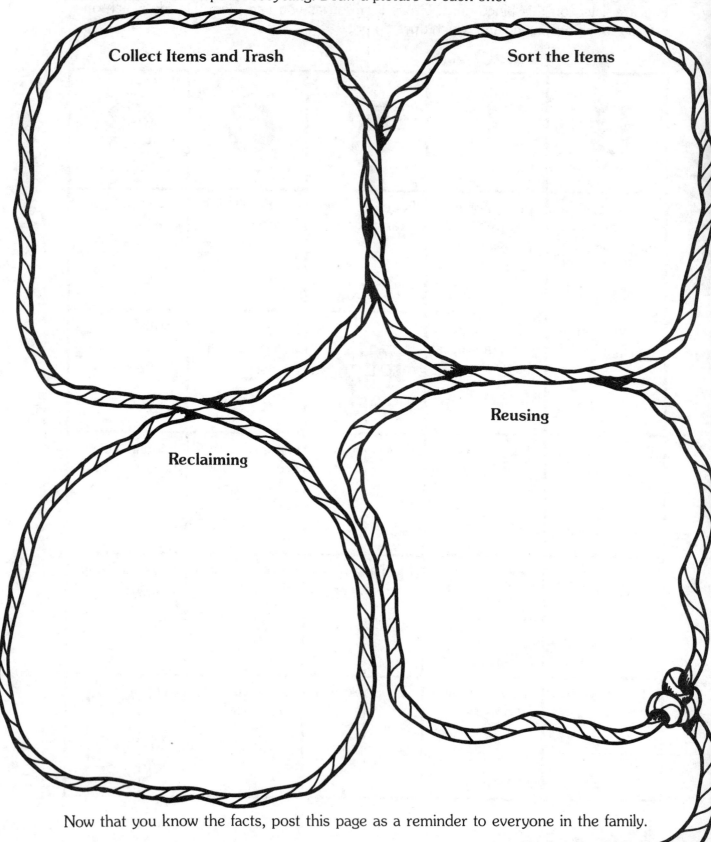

Collect Items and Trash

Sort the Items

Reclaiming

Reusing

Now that you know the facts, post this page as a reminder to everyone in the family.

292

The Wizard of Art

There's no place like home. Here's a chance to draw a picture of yours and list how you can save energy when you are in each room.

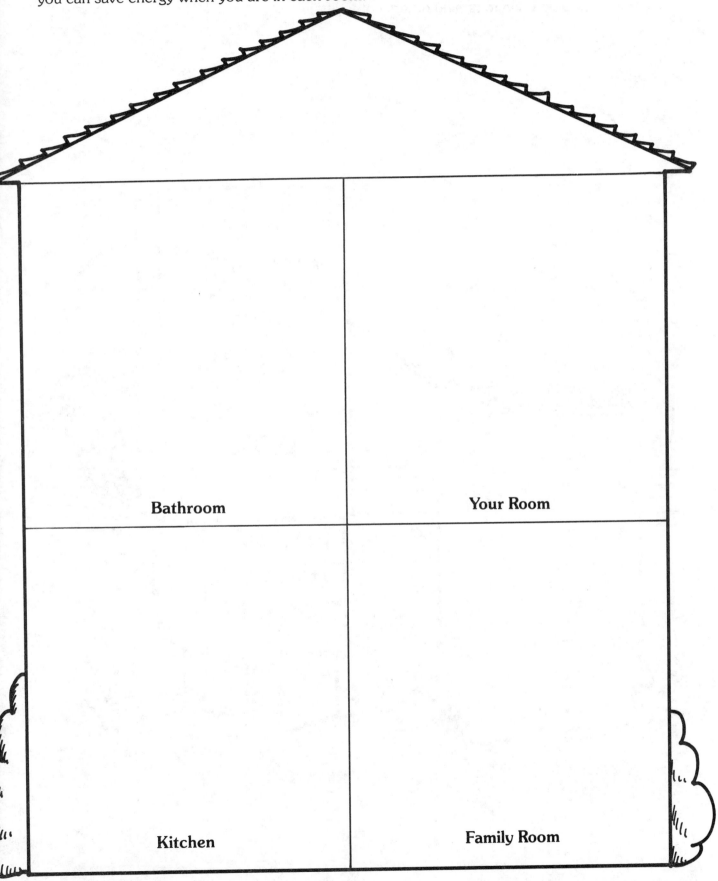

Bathroom

Your Room

Kitchen

Family Room

GA1342

Summer Sculpture

Collect trash on the beach. Build a mound of trash or a litterman. Post it near the trash can with a sign to remind others not to litter.

THROW AWAY TRASH!

GA1342

It "Bears" Repeating . . . .
Save Planet Earth!   Save Planet Earth!

Homonyms are words that sound the same but are spelled differently and have different meanings. Can you name the homonym for each of the following words and record its match?

ant _____

there _____

see _____

blue _____

week _____

right _____

tail _____

oar _____

do _____

pair _____

night _____

one _____

eye _____

meat _____

mail _____

be _____

flu _____

too _____

road _____

new _____

stair _____

when _____

so _____

sun _____

GA1342

Picture Perfect

Earth to Student: Pretend you have visited the most beautiful place on earth during your summer vacation. Write home and tell everyone about it!

Dear

To:

296

Soak Up These Facts

Be an advocate for planet Earth. In each drop, write a fact you want your family to know. Post the page in a place where everyone will see it.

Earth Addition

Complete the puzzle so that every number sentence is correct.

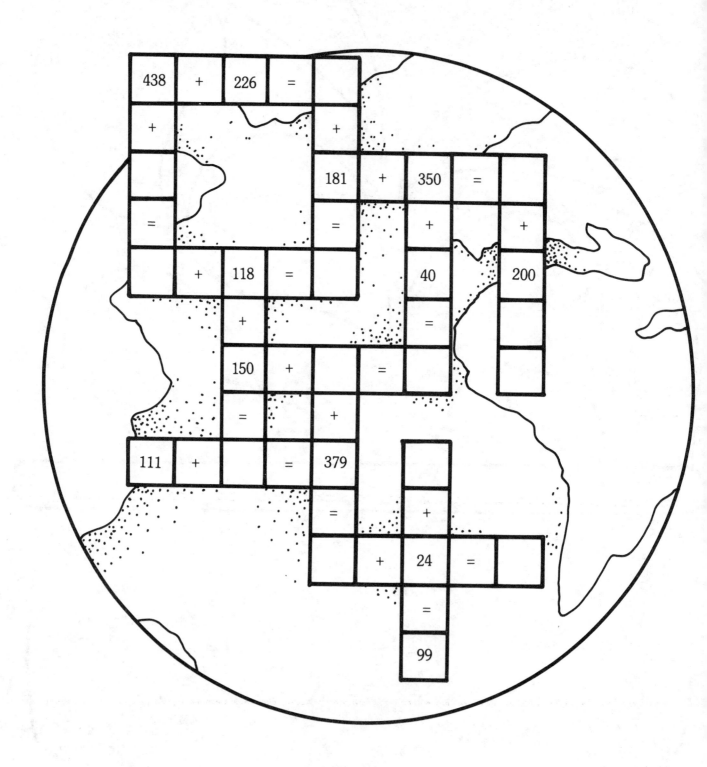

GA1342

Bumper to Bumper

Design a bumper sticker to remind others that they "auto" help the earth!

299

GA1342

Collection Connection

Anything you don't want is TRASH. *But* if something is of value to you, it is not trash even if other people throw it away. Do you have any collections?

What are some things people collect that others call trash? What would you like to collect?

For example:

I could collect:

Start a collection now. Some summer ideas are seashells, dried flowers, rocks. Remember the more you study about your collection, the more fun you will have.

How many words with three letters or more can you make out of

Environmental Alert

GA1342

Bike It

Riding bikes saves energy and is good exercise for you. Learn the bike riding laws in your community. Wear a helmet *always*. List all the places you can ride your bike to this summer.

1. _____
2. _____
3. _____
4. _____

Pick one. Draw a map below of the route you will ride from your house to your destination.

GA1342

Play It

It takes perseverance and concentration to take care of planet Earth. Make a concentration game. Cut out the squares below. Place them facedown on a table. With a friend, take turns trying to make a match.

recycle	recycle	energy	energy
environment	environment	earth	earth
biodegradable	biodegradable	resource	resource
plastic	plastic	aluminum	aluminum
species	species	paper	paper
coal	coal	oil	oil

GA1342

Picture a Postcard

Picture a summer scene that is as pretty as a postcard. Draw a picture of the place and write home to tell us all about it.

Dear

Here's what it looks like.

Your friend,

Imagine what these pretty scenes would look like if they were covered in litter?

Hi

Here's where I went.

From,

304

GA1342

More Trash to Treasures

Here are some super art ideas for turning throwaways into treasured items!

Meat Tray Magic

1. Draw a picture with a pencil on a meat tray. Either cut off the edges so it will be flat or use the bottom surface.

2. Paint the meat tray with tempera paint and if printing rollers are available, use them. Try to get a smooth coat of paint and avoid painting the embossed lines. Use a light coat of paint.

3. Place a piece of paper over the painted surface and press gently for contact. Lift the paper to reveal your design.

* For a new look, try water-base markers and color the design entirely. Repeat the same printing process.

305

GA1342

Summer Shapes

1. The  is in full bloom. As you walk through your yard or at the beach, how many shapes can you find in nature? What are they?

Shape	Found in Nature	Shape	Found in Nature
■		▲	
●		◆	

2. Trees come in many shapes and so do leaves. Collect three different shaped leaves and paste them below. Do you have a pointy leaf? One with lobes? What about one with pointed edges? Why do you think leaves come in different shapes?

GA1342

Glass Class

About 10 percent of the trash thrown away is glass. How many glass containers are in your pantry?

Here are two different sized containers and simple ideas to reuse them.

flower vase

container for candy, cotton balls, rice, etc.

Drink Bottle

Need: white glue, colored tissue paper, paintbrush

Water down the glue. Tear the colored tissue into small pieces. Cover the bottle with colored tissue, "painting" each piece in place with glue. Overlap the colored papers until the bottle is totally covered. Let dry thoroughly. You have a lovely new vase.

Jar with Lid

Need: yarn, glue, paintbrush, scrap of material cut into a circle larger than the lid

Beginning at the *bottom*, paint glue around the jar. Start at bottom, wrap yarn around jar, placing each row as close as possible to the row before.

Alternate painting glue and wrapping yarn until you reach the top. While jar dries, place lid facedown on cloth and then center. When placed, pick up lid and paint with glue. Put material in place. Circle lid with ribbon of yarn.

On the Go

Help keep America beautiful and design a trash bag for use in your car. Bring into class a small shopping bag that can be decorated with colorful scraps and personalized with your family's name. Draw a car border. Color the sign below and attach it to your bag.

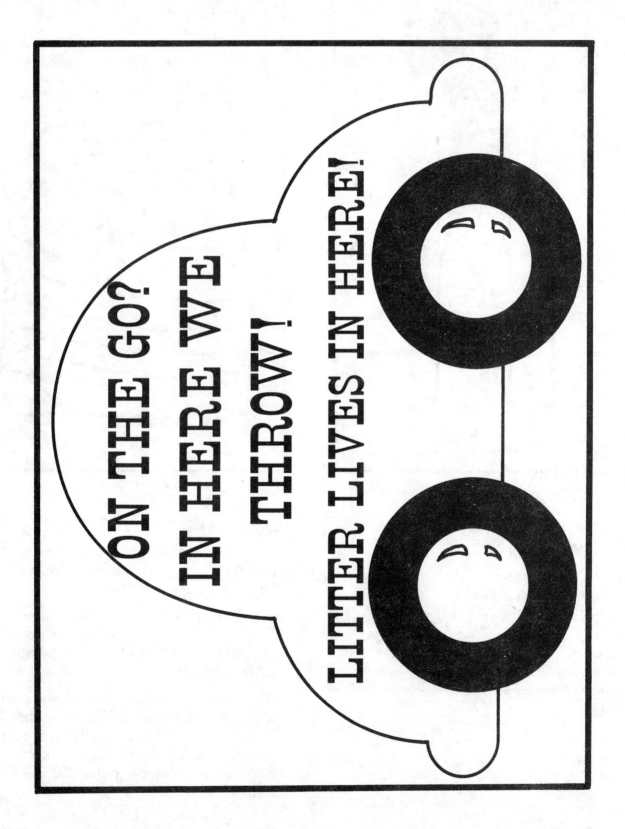

308

Did You Know?

If everyone recycled their newspapers, we could save 250,000,000 trees a year?

Each year Americans throw away enough writing paper and computer paper to build a wall 12 feet (3.64 m) high that stretches across the U.S.?

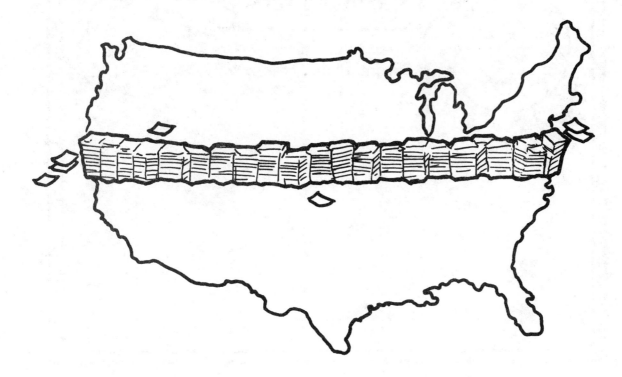

How many ways can you think of to reuse this piece of paper? Here are a few examples.

1. Give it to a friend to read.
2. Make a paper airplane.
3. Wrap a present in it?
4. _____
5. _____
6. _____
7. _____
8. _____
9. _____
10. _____

Think Recycle

GA1342

Send an Earth-a-Gram

Here's your chance to send a message to outer space and also one from outer space to planet Earth. What will your messages say?

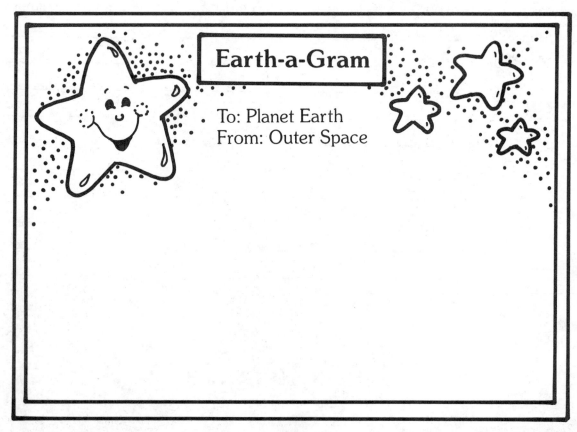

GA1342

Clean Up Your Act

Pesticides cannot be seen, smelled or tasted. In the summertime, many people spray more often for bugs. After spraying the house, it is very important to wash the counters and surfaces that come in contact with food.

Organically grown produce is grown without *pesticides* or *fungicides* or ripening chemicals like *alar*. When you shop with your parent next time, check the produce to see if it is organically grown or "alar free."

Ask the food produce manager at your favorite grocery story these questions:

1. Which foods are organically grown without chemicals?

   _____

   _____

   _____

2. Are any of the apples you sell alar free?

   _____

   _____

   _____

3. How do you suggest we make the produce we buy safe for eating?

   _____

   _____

   _____

GA1342

Bottle Notes

Here's a "classical" use for glass bottles. Instead of throwing them away, make a musical instrument. Collect ten or more glass bottles and jars of different sizes and shapes. When you blow in the bottles, what sounds do they make? Line up the clean bottles and jars on a table. Fill each with different amounts of water. Blow. How do the sounds change? Can you arrange the bottles from low notes to high? Can you play a song?

GA1342

Earth Hero

You've been working hard. Give yourself an award. Cut out the shape below, color and decorate. Wear your badge proudly until you see another Earth Hero. Award it to someone who is taking care of planet Earth. Ask this Earth Hero to proudly wear the badge until he/she finds someone to pass it on to.

GA1342

What on Earth You Can Do with Kids

Holiday Helpers

314

A Worldly Welcome

September

S	M	T	W	T	F	S
	1	2	3	4	5	6
7	8	9	10	11	12	13
14	15	16	17	18	19	20
21	22	23	24	25	26	27
28	29	30	31			

Reuse this calendar each month with a different theme to focus on the monthly topics. Here are some timely topics to enhance your effort. The calendar can be made from a sheet of white poster board to prevent fading. Patterns can be duplicated with one for each day of the month and the correct calendar day and date as shown above.

September	Have Fun in Fall
October	October Will Spellbound You!
November	November Remembers the Earth
December	Decide to Help in December
January	There's "Snow" Time to Help like the Present!
February	Hearty Helpers in February
March	March Treasures the Earth
April	Be "Hoppy" to Help in April
May	Movers and Shakers in May

Calendar Companion

1 2 3
4 5 6 7 8
9 10 11
12 13 14
15 16 17

GA1342

18 19 20
21 22 23
24 25 26
27 28 29
30 31

GA1342

September Holiday Helpers

First Monday in September—Labor Day. What is Labor Day? How do you labor? Who labors to help planet Earth? Who are the earth's helpers?

September 19, 1928—Mickey Mouse first appeared in a talking cartoon. Who created Mickey Mouse? Is a mouse an endangered species? Can you name any?

September 23—First day of autumn. Look around you. What signs of autumn do you see? How is the earth changing?

First Saturday after the full moon—American Indian Day. How did the Indians help and use the earth? Why do we have American Indian Day? Watch for the first full moon and record its date.

September 25—First American newspaper was published in 1690. Look in the newspaper for current events about the earth. Add them to the calendar. September is also American Newspaper Week. Invite a reporter to class to discuss his career.

September 26—In 1774 Johnny Appleseed was born. How did he help the earth by spreading seeds and planting trees? His real name was John Chapman. How did he get the name "Appleseed"?

September is also National Sight-Saving Month and Read-a-New-Book Month. Each time a student reads a book, he is recycling. Add his name to the bulletin board. Encourage students to read books that relate to the environment.

Sukkot—The Feast of Tabernacles, the Jewish festival occurring in September or October. What is a succot and how is it used?

Simhat Torah—A Jewish holiday that occurs after Sukkot. It celebrates rejoicing with the torah and is a festive day.

GA1342

Headliner Happening

Celebrate American Newspaper Week and have a birthday party for the first newspaper which was published in 1690 on September 25th. Any story appearing in a newspaper should answer the five important facts who, what, when, where and why. Be a reporter and write your ideas to complete this story!

Earth Day Is Every Day!

Who _____

_____

_____

_____

What _____

_____

_____

_____

When _____

_____

_____

_____

Where _____

_____

_____

_____

Why _____

_____

_____

_____

Don't Forget to Recycle Your Newspapers!

GA1342

Scrambled Earth

Explore the globe and find where you live. Then locate new countries and scramble their letters and list them on this page. Exchange papers with a classmate and challenge him to unscramble the words and spell the countries or places correctly.

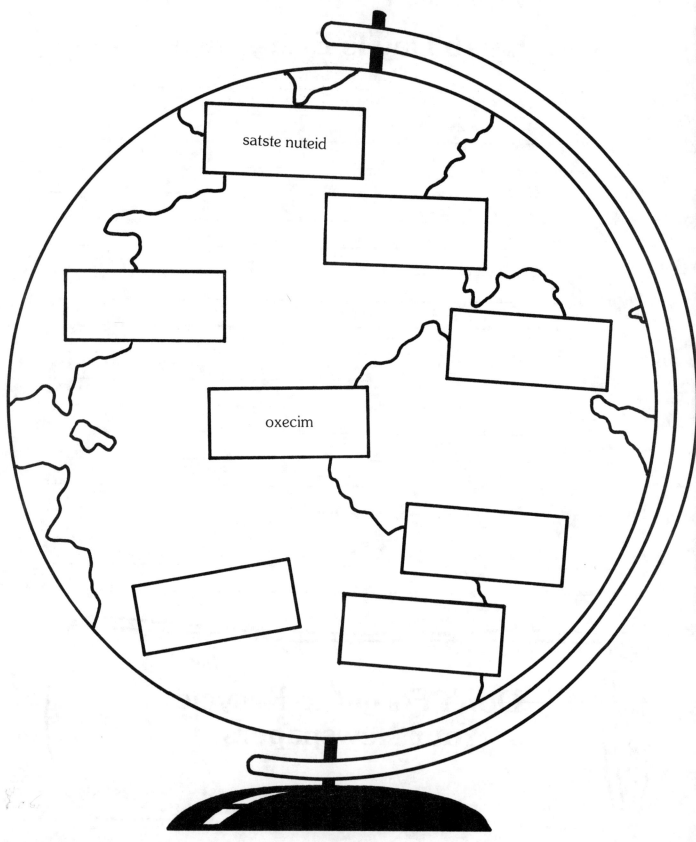

satste nuteid

oxecim

GA1342

October Holiday Helpers

October 1—First World Series played in 1903. What is the World Series and why is it called that?

October 2—Grandparents' Day. Interview your grandparent or an elderly neighbor and find out how the environment has changed since he/she was younger.

October 9—Leif Ericson Day. Who was Leif Ericson?

October 15—National Poetry Day. Write a poem about the earth.

October 24—United Nations Day. How have nations united to help the earth? How do you think they could help?

On October 28—The Statue of Liberty was dedicated. How has the environment hurt the Statue of Liberty? What was done to help it?

October 31—Halloween. How can you "treat" the earth so that it won't be tricked? Make a list of earth treats!

Fire Prevention Week is also in October. How can you help prevent fires? Who and what contributes to forest fires?

Rosh Hashanah occurs in September or October and ushers in the Jewish New Year.

Yom Kippur is the Jewish holiday called the Day of Atonement and is a day of fasting and prayer.

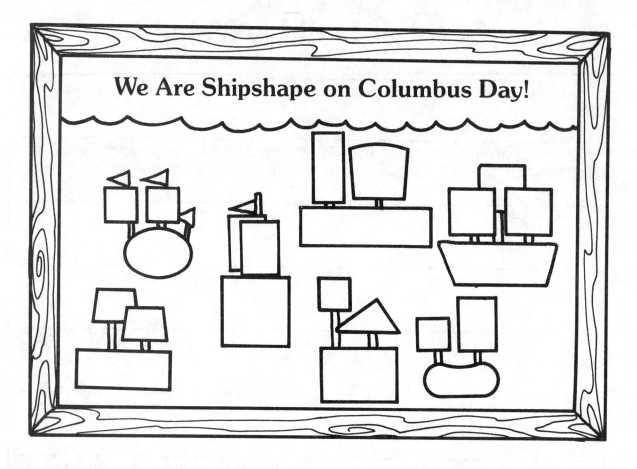

We Are Shipshape on Columbus Day!

Use this bulletin board to celebrate Columbus Day. Teach students the age-old saying "In 1492 Columbus sailed the ocean blue . . . ."

To create Columbus Day ships, give each student a piece of blue construction paper, glue, scissors and an assortment of shapes. Have an art activity where students glue all the shapes to help Columbus sail in a shipshape ship!

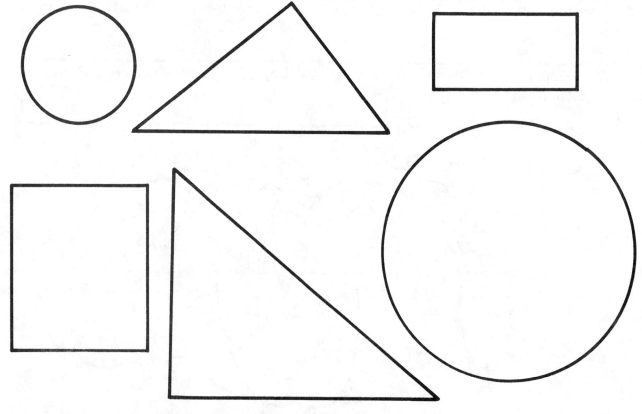

GA1342

October Designs

This year, how about making your Halloween costume from recycled items? Search your home for things you could use and discuss with your family how these items could be combined to make a costume.

Draw a picture of your idea here.

Some ideas include making a vest out of a brown bag and using Mom's or Dad's old clothes to make a new look for you!

GA1342

November Holiday Helpers

First Tuesday after the first Monday in November—Election Day. Cast your vote for a healthy planet. Write politicians and tell them how you feel.

November 9—Sadie Hawkins Day. Do you know what this is?

November 13—In 1890 peanut butter was invented. What other foods are "recycled" and made into new, edible products?

November 14—Favorite Author's Day. Find an author who has written a book to help the earth.

November 18—Mickey Mouse's Birthday. Like Mickey, be all ears and listen for ways you can help the environment.

Fourth Thursday—Thanksgiving. Be thankful for our beautiful planet, trees, flowers. Make a list of all the things you feel we should be thankful for.

Special event in November also includes Children's Book Week—Report on a book you have read that might help the earth. Be an author and write a story yourself!

Good Nutrition Month. As you eat healthy, nutritious foods, make sure you clean them properly before eating. What foods must be washed? How long do they stay fresh? Can you list ideas for developing healthy habits?

Third Monday—National Stamp Collecting. Save the stamps from junk mail and start a stamp collection. Compare your stamps with fellow students and see if you can make a match. Add up the total sum of all of your stamps.

American Education Week. Research education in America and find out how and when schools began. Write a thank-you note to a teacher to express your feelings of appreciation for helping you learn.

GA1342

My Stamp of Approval

Stamp collecting is a fun and interesting hobby. Draw a picture of two of your favorite stamps and then design some of your own to highlight the earth and how important it is to help save its treasures. Send your ideas to the U.S. Postal Service.

GA1342

Gobble Up These Facts!

Disposable Diapers don't dispose!

Plastic water...

Plastic cups don't decompose

A ten-minute shower uses 100 gallons of water

Deforestation is the complete destruction of all the tr...

A leaky faucet can drip 50 gallons of water a d...

Eagles and pandas are endangered

A microwave oven uses 1/3 to 1/2 the energy of a conventional!

throw away millions of razor blades!

(and do something about them!)

Get down to earth and encourage your students during the month of November to change the facts about planet Earth so we can be thankful. Ask students to cover each old feather with a new one with a new solution.

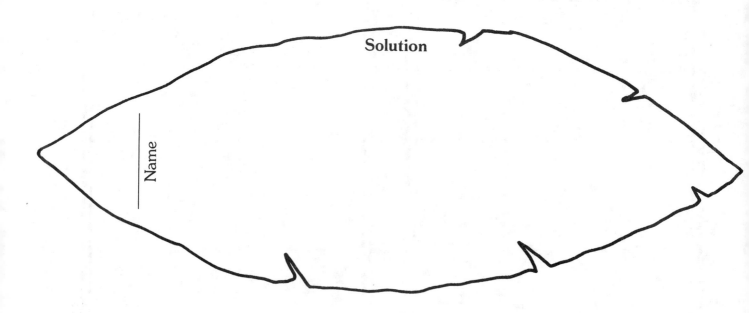

Solution

Name

326

December Holiday Helpers

December—First gas station opened in Pittsburgh, 1913. How does gas get to a gas station and where does it come from?

December 2—Georges Seurat, French painter, born in 1859. Write a report on any artist who painted landscapes. Paint a painting of an outdoor scene. How would it change each season?

December 7—Pearl Harbor Day, 1941

December 8—Eli Whitney, inventor of cotton gin, born in 1765. How did this invention help mankind?

December 10—First Nobel Prize awarded in 1901. Why are Nobel Prizes important? What discovery or invention would help the earth?

December 16—Ludwig van Beethoven born in 1770. What animals in nature make music? Do you think musicians listen to nature?

December 25—Christmas Day. How do the customs of Christmas differ throughout the world? How can we save trees?

Hanukkah—Begins in the eve of the twenty-fifth day of the Hebrew month, Kislev. The Festival of Lights lasts eight days. What light lasted eight days and why?

December 31—Harry S. Truman, U.S. President announced the official end of World War II in 1946.

GA1342

December De"lights"

December is a festive month full of delightful holidays and things that delight us, from the lights on Christmas trees to the Hanukkah candles that shed light each night to the delighted faces as presents are exchanged. December is definitely de**light**ful! Have a class discussion about ways you can delight the earth. From saving energy to considering gifts for our planet, encourage students to list their ideas on the light bulbs below. Color them in and they can be added to create a delightful bulletin board border.

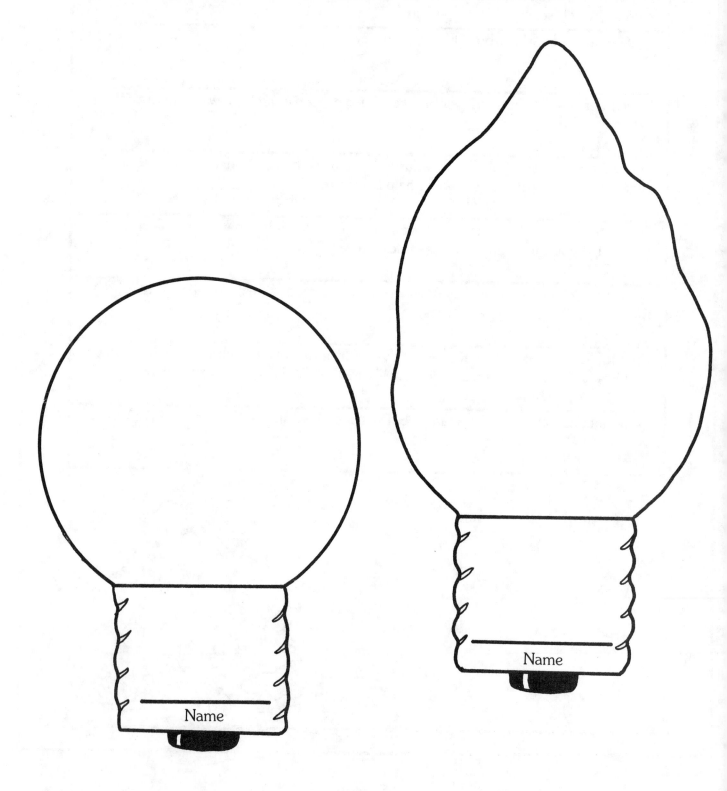

328

GA1342

Wrap It Up!

Think of a variety of ways you can help recycle and cut down on trash during the holiday season. Draw your gift wrapping ideas here.

Make your own gift wrap by decorating brown paper, newspaper or another type of paper.

GA1342

Paper Plate Pizzaz

Paper plates can be used in a variety of ways. Here are some super ideas ideal for holiday happenings.

Valentine Holder

Cut a paper plate in half and staple it together.

September Parade Shake, Rattle and Roll

Fill two paper plates with popcorn seeds or bottle caps. Staple the paper plates front side to front. Shake it for a fun musical instrument.

Decorate the exterior with magic markers, stickers, etc.

Some "Bunny" Likes You

Use a paper plate to make a bunny rabbit for Easter. Color the face, add a pipe cleaner nose and paper ears. A body can also be created from a paper plate.

April Sunshine Chart

Each time you do a good deed for the earth, add a ray of sunshine by drawing a line to a smiling paper plate.

Punch holes in a paper plate and with an old shoelace make a sewing card for a younger sibling or friend.

December Gift Wrap

Decorate a paper plate on the bottom and do the same for a matching plate. Staple the plates together and put your gift inside before stapling all the sides securely. This is a super gift wrap.

GA1342

"Elf" You Recycle. . .You'll Help the Earth!

Use this bulletin board during the holiday season to encourage recycling. Have students collect used ribbons, bows, gift wrap paper and gift tags from presents or previous special occasions. Each student can make a gift package by collaging the scraps and items together to make a present. Each present should use a variety of gift paper patterns and be as exciting and colorful as possible. Students can write clues on index cards about what's inside their presents and challenge each other to guess what's inside.

It's furry, alive, sweet, small and friendly.

It's round, fun, can bounce and is soft.

GA1342

January Holiday Helpers

January 1—New Year's Day. Write a universal New Year's resolution that you think everyone on earth should sign.

January 1—Betsy Ross born in 1752. What was Betsy Ross famous for?

January 4—Louis Braille born in 1809.

January 8—Elvis Presley born in 1935.

January 15—Martin Luther King, Jr., born in 1929.

January 20—Inauguration Day. Every fourth year the President of the U.S. takes the oath of office on this day. What oath should be included that would help planet Earth?

January 27—Wolfgang Amadeus Mozart born in 1756.

January 30—Franklin D. Roosevelt born in 1882.

GA1342

New Year's Resolution

As an Earthling, I resolve that every time I shop I will ask these questions:

1. ☐ Do we really need this?

2. ☐ Is the package recyclable or returnable?

3. ☐ Is there another product that does the same thing but is better for the environment?

4. ☐ If the product is disposable, can I find a way to reuse it?

5. ☐ Is there a nondisposable alternative?

6. ☐ Can I use this product a number of times before I will have to throw it away?

7. ☐ Is this product repairable?

8. ☐ Could I borrow this instead of buying it?

9. ☐ When I throw this away will it hurt the environment?

Earth to Home: Share this list with Mom and Dad.

Tip: Check your used cereal boxes. If the cardboard inside is gray or tan, it's been made from *recycled* paper. If you like the cereal, that's one more reason to buy it!

GA1342

I Have a Dream. . . .

Martin Luther King, Jr., is a very famous black American. One of his most famous speeches began, "I have a dream. . . ." His dream was that all men would be able to live together in peace. He dreamed and hoped that all men would be judged not by the color of their skin but by the content of their character. What dream do you have for planet Earth? Post the students' ideas.

"I have a dream . . . ."

Earth to Student: Plan a one-minute "I have a dream . . ." speech to give to the class.

GA1342

February Holiday Helpers

February 1—National Freedom Day. How have we abused our freedom on earth, and how can we change?

February 2—Groundhog Day. Why is the groundhog important to the earth?

February 3—National League of baseball was organized in 1876. How can mankind bat a thousand for planet Earth? What ideas might score a run to help Earth win the game?

February 11—Thomas Alva Edison born in 1847. What would life be like without Edison's discovery?

February 12—Abraham Lincoln born in 1809.

February 14—Valentine's Day. How many heartwarming ways can you think of that would be good deeds for the earth?

February 22—George Washington born in 1732. George Washington chopped down a cherry tree and told the truth about it. What things have you done that you can change in order to help save the earth's treasures?

February 29—Leap Year Day occurs every four years.

Afro-American History Month

Purim occurs in February or March. Jewish holiday Feast of Lots.

National Wildlife Week—Third Sunday in February. How can you help wildlife around you?

GA1342

A Penny for Your Thoughts

Abraham Lincoln was born on February 12, 1809. How did he help when he was President? If you were President, how would you help the earth?

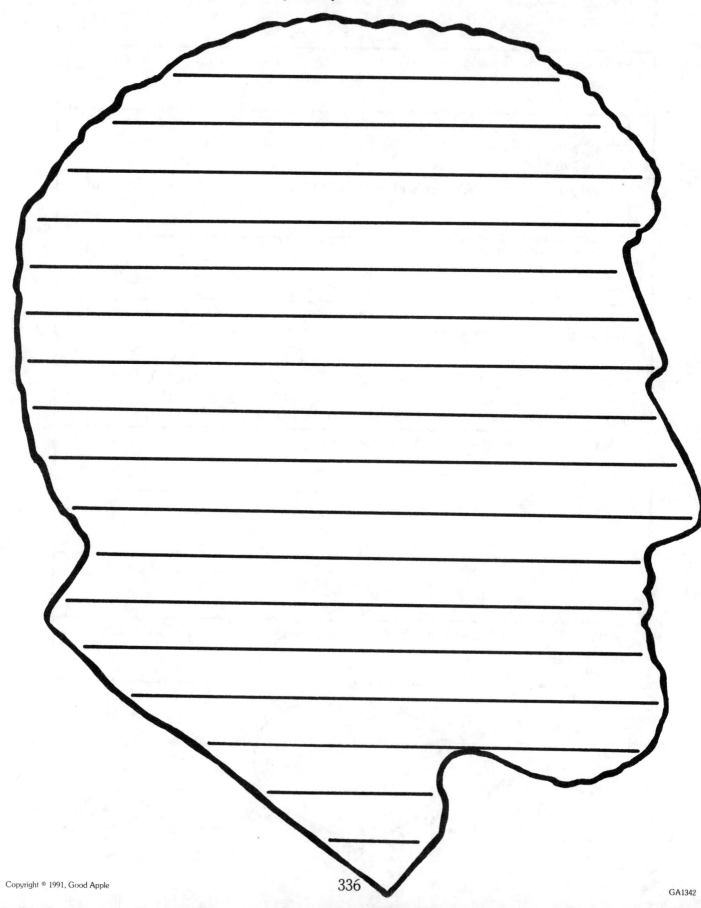

GA1342

A Valentine from Earth

Use my code to decode my message to you. Happy Valentine's Day!

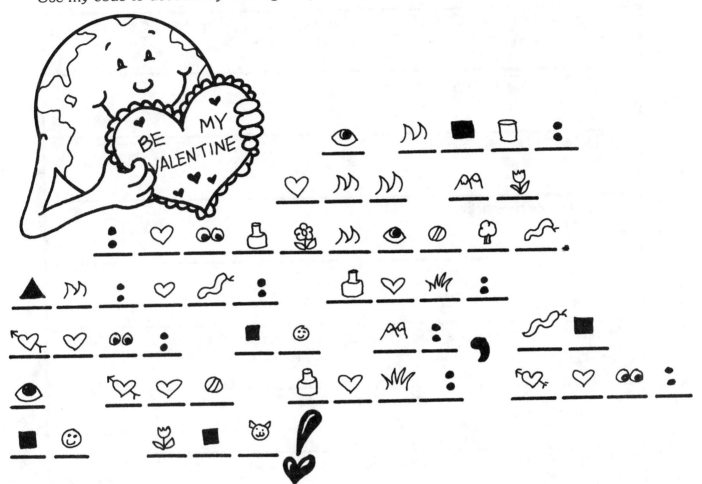

GA1342

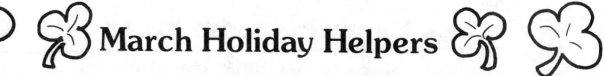

March Holiday Helpers

March 1—First United States Bank established in 1780. What ideas do you think we can bank on to help the earth?

March 3—Doll Festival in Japan

March 4—Dr. Seuss's birthday

March 6—Michelangelo born in 1475.

March 17th—St. Patrick's Day

March 21—First day of spring. How will you change how you dress now that spring has arrived? What changes will occur besides how you dress?

March 26—Robert Frost, American poet born in 1874.

March is also National Nutrition Week.

Save Your Vision Week.

Camp Fire Girls Week—Interview a Camp Fire Girl and find out how Camp Fire Girls are helping to care for the environment?

Red Cross Month

Youth Art Month

March 1—National Weight and Measures Week

GA1342

Go Fly a Kite!

Use this bulletin board to celebrate the month of March with a recycling art project. Create a scrap box by saving paper, scraps, wallpaper, etc. Each student will enjoy creating an assemblage with the colorful odds and ends to make a kite. This is also a perfect opportunity to discuss wind and energy. Use the pattern below and duplicate one for each student. As students fly high in their studies and do good work, advance their kites up an inch (centimeter) or two. The object is to sail your kite to the top of the bulletin board.

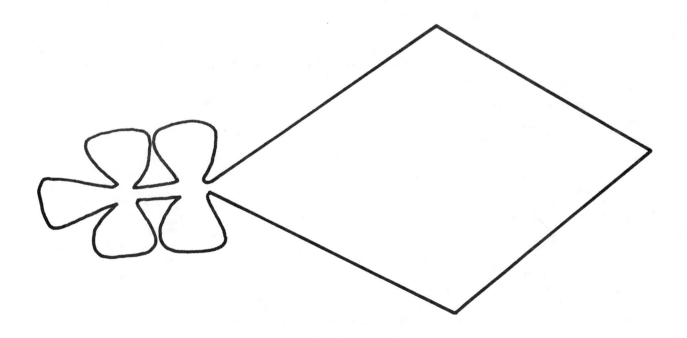

The Green Scene

The official color of St. Patrick's Day is green. Do you know why?

Make a list of everything that you can think of that's green and record it here.

Money is green. How can you save money and protect the earth? What products should you boycott?

April Holiday Helpers

April 1—April Fool's Day
April 2—International Children's Book Day. Hans Christian Andersen born in 1805.
April 6—Harry Houdini born in 1874.
April 10—First Arbor Day
April 18—Anniversary of Paul Revere's Ride in 1775.
April 22—Earth Day
April 23—William Shakespeare born in 1564.
Also in April—Passover: feast of unleavened bread. Jewish holiday beginning on fifteenth day of Nisan and occurs in March or April.
Good Friday—Friday before Easter
Easter
Olympics began in Athens, Greece, in 1896.
National Library Week
National Automobile Month

GA1342

A Tisket, a Tasket,
Recycle Your Easter Basket!

Baskets can be redecorated and reused over and over again. Here are some recycling tips.

Cut a milk carton into a basket shape. A grown-up can help you cut it.

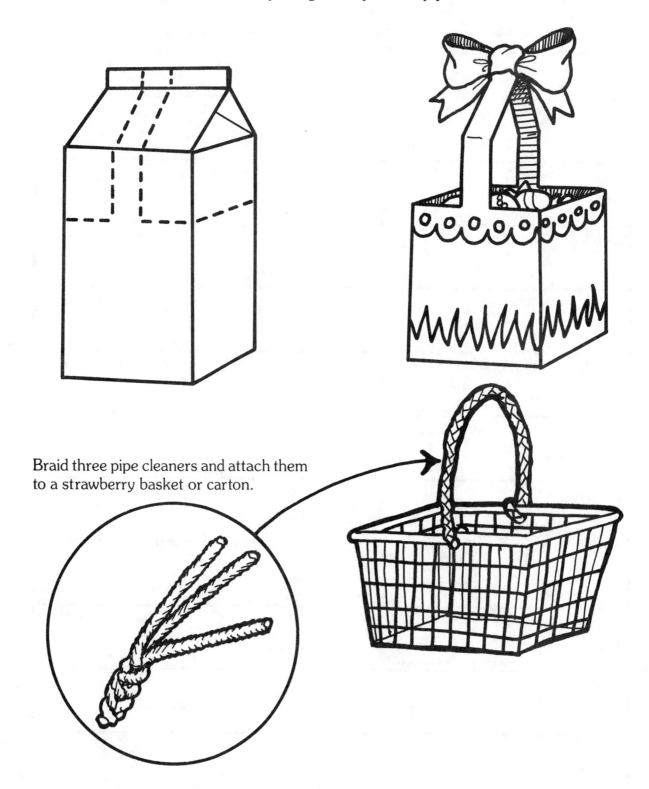

Braid three pipe cleaners and attach them to a strawberry basket or carton.

342

GA1342

Here's a bulletin board that is no joke. Have students make up earth-saving riddles to stump their classmates. Of course since everyone is "up" on planet Earth, no one will get stumped!

One starter is:
Why did the little elephant hide his tusks? (. . .to save his skin!)

May Holiday Helpers

May 1—May Day
May 6—World's first postage stamp issued in 1840.
May 7—Red Cross Day
May 8—Harry S. Truman's birthday
2nd Sunday—Mother's Day
May 15—Frank Baum born in 1856.
May 21—Clara Barton, founder of the American Red Cross, born in 1881.
May 29—John F. Kennedy's birthday
Last Monday in May—Memorial Day
Also in May: Be Kind to Animals Week
National Music Week
National Metric Week

GA1342

Greatest Mom on Earth!

Draw a portrait of your mom or write a letter to her and list why she's the greatest mom on earth and you are the luckiest kid! List one thing she's taught you that's made you a conscientious earthling.

GA1342

Father's Day Fun

Write a letter to your dad, grandpa or a favorite father of a friend and tell him why he's special.

On the tie list the things Dad has taught you that make the earth a better place to live.

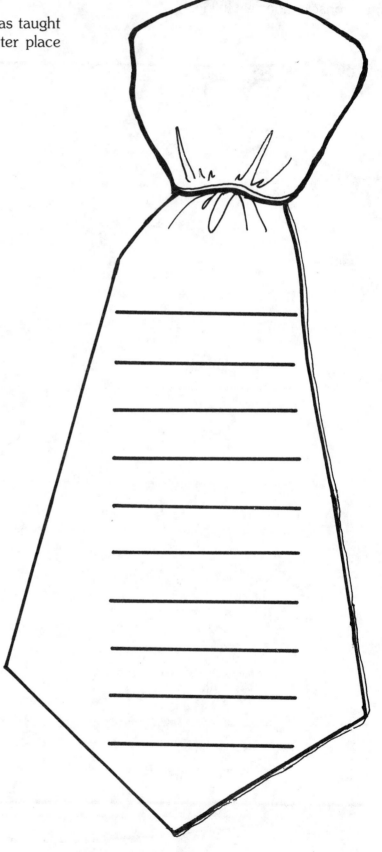

346

Made in the U.S.A.

July 4th: On July 4th, think about all the things that you have or know about that are made in the U.S.A. List them below.

GA1342

Month-by-Month Recycling

Pick a used page of a calendar and . . .

Add up all the horizontal rows.

Circle all the even numbers.

Add up all the vertical rows.

Circle all the odd numbers.

January

S	M	T	W	TH	F	S
	1	2	3	4	5	6
7	8	9	10	11	12	13
14	15	16	17	18	19	20
21	22	23	24	25	26	27
28	29	30	31			

Cross off all the numbers that add up to 4. Circle the numbers that when added equal 3.

Circle your favorite day last month. What did you do?